APC: Your p
guide to s

C000174738

Christina Hirst

RICS | the mark of property professionalism worldwide

Published by the Royal Institution of Chartered Surveyors (RICS)
Surveyor Court
Westwood Business Park
Coventry CV4 8JE
UK
www.ricsbooks.com

First edition published 2001
Second edition published 2003, reprinted 2005
Third edition published 2006

ISBN 978 1 84219 490 4

Typeset in Great Britain by Columns Design Ltd, Reading, Berks

Printed in Great Britain by Page Bros, Milecross Lane, Norwich

Contents

Foreword

In July 2006, RICS launched a revised APC, which incorporated many improvements to the competencies and guidance. This has been further enhanced with the upgrade of the APC templates in December 2008. This positive change is not only beneficial to candidates but is also designed to provide assessment panels with more concise information about a candidate's training and experience, allowing them to plan their interview questions more easily from the pre-submission documents.

RICS training adviser Christina Hirst looks at these changes in detail whilst retaining much of the helpful advice that was included in the previous editions of this publication.

I believe this book complements the official APC guidance produced by RICS and is a useful supplement for any candidate undertaking the APC. It will also be a valuable resource for employers, supervisors and counsellors.

Suzanne Roberts

Membership Operations

Preface

When I was asked to update this book I felt this was a great opportunity for me to build on the excellent work of the original author, John Wilkinson, but also to take the opportunity to reflect the many changes that have taken place to the APC since its publication and to reflect current best practice. The aim of the book is to give you guidance to help steer you through your APC from the very beginning of your period of structured training to your success at the final assessment. I would just point out that the objective of this book is not to replace the RICS formal guidance but to supplement this. The APC by its very nature must be dynamic and must adapt to reflect changes in the work and practice of surveyors; therefore, you should ensure that you follow the up to date guidance published by RICS at www.rics.org/apc. The contact details page at the back of the book will help point you in the right direction for this and other formal information.

I have been involved with the APC as an RICS training adviser for over ten years now and during that time have met many different candidates working in a vast range of different organisations. There are a number of useful tips that all candidates seem to agree on:

● Keep up to date with your APC diary and templates.

● Make sure you understand the requirements from the outset.

- Manage your supervisor and counsellor!
- Ask if you are not sure – the hardest question to answer is the one that starts 'this may be a daft question...'!

This book will help you address these and more.

The APC pathways and competencies have been developed and agreed by practising surveyors within the different professional groups. They are intended to reflect the work of surveyors within the particular specialisms. Generally you will find that your day to day work will allow you to meet the necessary competencies but if you feel this would be difficult to achieve discuss this with your supervisor and counsellor when agreeing your training plan. There are many different ways that additional experience can be obtained, including working with others in your organisation or taking a secondment. You should never feel that it is not possible to succeed in your APC – where there is a will there is a way.

I would urge you to project manage your APC. Take time out to set an action plan for yourself and set time aside each week to do your diary much in the same way as you will have set time aside for your studies. Think of the APC as a qualification – little and often is usually a good approach to studying. Don't leave everything until the very end – choose your critical analysis project early and use your professional development to help you to develop the necessary additional knowledge you may need.

The APC will take time and effort but the rewards are immense – chartered surveyors truly are the gold standard in the property and construction professions. Good luck with your APC and best wishes for a long, prosperous and successful surveying career.

Christina Hirst

APC overview

This chapter provides an overview of the basic philosophies and key concepts of the APC, as well as an introduction to the guidance documents and templates and a note of relevant dates and deadlines. It also outlines the roles and responsibilities of some of the people essential to your training and development, such as RICS training advisers (RTAs), APC doctors, your employer and RICS itself.

Routes to membership

There are various 'routes' which will lead you to chartered membership of RICS, including:

- **Graduate route 1** – for those with an RICS accredited degree and less than five years relevant surveying experience;

- **Graduate route 2** – for those with an RICS accredited degree and between five and ten years relevant surveying experience (this may include pre-degree experience);

- **Graduate route 3** – for those with an RICS accredited degree and ten-years or more relevant surveying experience (this may include pre-degree experience);

- **Adaptation route** – for those with either an RICS approved professional body membership or non accredited but relevant degree and nine years relevant surveying experience. Candidates for this route must complete 450 study hours from an RICS accredited degree either at postgraduate level, from the final year of an undergraduate degree or from an approved training provider;

• **Academic** – for those who hold a surveying related higher degree and have undertaken academic activities on an RICS accredited degree over a three year period or who hold an RICS accredited degree and have undertaken academic activities relating to the profession over a three year period; and

• **Senior professional** – for professionals who are now in a **senior** industry position and hold a surveying related degree and have more than five years surveying experience.

Linked to the routes are a series of APC 'pathways' and before you begin the APC you must choose, in consultation with your employer, an APC pathway appropriate to the work experience you will be able to obtain. The pathway chosen will lead you to membership of one of the RICS professional groups.

This book aims to guide you along graduate routes 1 and 2, although chapter 5 will also be useful for candidates on graduate route 3.

Official guidance

This book does not intend to repeat the contents of the RICS APC guidance. It is therefore essential that you read and study the guidance available at www.rics.org/apc. You should also be aware that this book focuses on version 2/December 2008 of the APC guidance; however, you must keep up to date with any changes that are published by RICS and, most importantly, watch out for any transitional arrangements that may occur. Guidance is provided for candidates, supervisors, counsellors and employers with the aim of helping candidates through the APC and helping employers support their candidates. Above all, for employers the guidance outlines the commitment needed – it is important that your employer not only has a copy of the guidance, but is fully aware of his or her responsibilities. You might like to give them a little encouragement to read it!

Guidance on the APC pathways has been written by experienced practitioners and aims to give a clear and practical understanding of how to apply the listed core and optional competencies in the context of your specific pathway and area of work. The official competency definitions (at levels one, two and three) are provided, followed by a description of the key knowledge and activities that are likely to fall within the scope of each competency. An example is provided in chapter 2 on page 20.

What is the APC?

The Assessment of Professional Competence (APC) is the process by which RICS seeks to be satisfied that candidates who wish to become members of the Institution are competent to practise as chartered surveyors.

To demonstrate this competence, candidates will undergo a rigorous and demanding period of structured training, over a minimum period of 23 calendar months, in which they must gain a minimum of 400 days of relevant work experience as well as undertake additional professional development. (For graduate route 2 candidates, the minimum requirement is 11 months and 200 days of relevant experience.) The objective is to enable the knowledge and theory gained primarily in higher education to be complemented by practical experience. The second part of the APC process is then the final assessment interview.

The APC therefore comprises two components:

1 *a period of structured training*: during this period you should keep a record, in a diary, of experience gained. You must also keep a candidate achievement record (see page 53) and an experience record (see page 54). The training period also incorporates your professional development, an outline of which is given later in this chapter (see also page 44);

2 *the final assessment interview*: a panel of a minimum of two assessors (although this panel will normally comprise three practitioners) will interview you over a period of one hour, and form a judgment, or 'assess', whether you are competent to practise as a member of RICS. (See page 60).

You should think of the APC as the practical training and experience which, when added to the study normally carried out at university, leads to membership of RICS (illustrated by figure 1).

STUDY AND LEARNING	+	APC	=	MRICS
Which may take place at university		Practical training and experience for a minimum period of either one or two years (graduate routes 2 and 1 respectively)		Membership of RICS

Figure 1 Route to membership of RICS

The APC can commence at a number of points depending upon your circumstances. For a graduate route 1 candidate these include:

- after you have graduated from an RICS accredited degree;

- at the commencement of a 'year out' placement from an RICS accredited sandwich degree;

- at the commencement of the final year of a part time or distance learning RICS accredited undergraduate degree; and

- at the commencement of the penultimate year of a part time or distance learning RICS accredited post graduate degree.

The starting points for graduate route 2 candidates are often later as you will already have more than 5 years experience on starting the APC.

The APC is a process of continuous assessment culminating in the final assessment by the RICS panel of assessors. Many candidates tend to focus on the final assessment only but you must firstly satisfy your supervisor and counsellor of your competence before you are able to go forward to the final assessment. At the final assessment the panel will consider:

- the depth and breadth of your training;

- the quality of your documents and written reports (including the critical analysis and candidate experience record); and

- your presentation at the interview.

At the end of the interview the panel will view your training and development with a holistic view of performance.

Key concepts and documents

Competent to practise

The APC is foremost a period of structured training and practical experience, which culminates in the final assessment interview, the objective of which is to assess your 'competence to practise', in other words your competence to carry out the work of a qualified surveyor. To be 'competent' is to have the skill or knowledge to carry out a task or function successfully. This ability can vary from being merely able, to being expert in a particular sphere of activity.

The APC requires you to achieve various competencies relevant to your APC pathway. The competencies are a mix of technical, professional and personal skills and come in three different categories:

1 mandatory competencies;

2 core competencies; and

3 optional competencies.

As you progress through the APC you will need to demonstrate to your supervisor and counsellor, and ultimately the final assessment panel, that you meet with the knowledge requirements of your chosen pathway. In addition, you will need to demonstrate the practical application of this knowledge and the ability to solve problems. You will also need to show that you have been developing the range of knowledge and skills required in the mandatory competencies, which comprise a mix of professional practice and interpersonal, business and management skills that are considered common to, and necessary for, all surveyors.

You will note that there is most importantly a focus on testing that you are aware of and intend to act in accordance with the RICS Rules of Conduct and that you understand the importance of ethics and professional practice matters. There is a specific guidance note on the Rules of Conduct for APC candidates, supervisors and counsellors further reinforcing the importance of this area. This is available at www.rics.org/apc

A competency

A competency is a statement of the skills or abilities required to perform a specific task or function. It is based upon attitudes and behaviours, as well as skills and knowledge. For the APC, the requirements and level of attainment for each pathway are set out in the APC guidance. Chapter 2 provides details specific competencies and shows how, at the final assessment, these will be drawn together by the assessment panel to form a holistic judgment of your competence to practise.

Structured training

'Structured training' is, as its name suggests, a structured approach to the delivery of training and experience over a given period. It is mandatory for all firms registering new APC candidates to have an approved structured training agreement in place. A template for use by employers in developing a structured training agreement can be downloaded from www.rics.org/apc

The structured training agreement is an agreement between your employer and RICS that formalises your employer's intended policy in implementing the RICS requirements for the APC. You will find more detail on this document in chapter 2.

There is no minimum requirement of training days to be completed under each competency, other than the overall requirement of the structured training period. For graduate route 1 this is a minimum of 400 days within

23 calendar months and for graduate route 2 this is a minimum of 200 days within 11 calendar months.

There is no specified period of structured training for graduate route 3.

An employer's structured training agreement must be approved by an RICS training advisor (RTA) – contact details of all RTAs are available at www.rics.org/apc. Once approved by your RTA, your employer will be listed on www.rics.org as having an approved structured training agreement.

APC templates

All the templates you will need for your APC are available on the RICS website (www.rics.org/apc). With the exception of the diary template these are all included within an Excel workbook for your specific pathway.

Diary

The diary is a day-to-day record of how you have been building your experience. The detail contained in it will assist you in completing your candidate achievement record (log book) and your experience record.

Candidate achievement record

The candidate achievement record includes what is known as the log book.

In this record you will give a monthly summary of the entries in your diary and provide a total of the number of days of experience gained in each of the competencies.

The candidate achievement record also charts your progress against the competency requirements of your chosen pathway using the log book summary. In other words, it is a record of your competency achievements as assessed by your supervisor and counsellor.

Professional development

Another important aspect of the training period is the requirement for you to undertake a minimum of 48 hours of professional development per annum. This is to provide you with the opportunity to gain knowledge and skills that might not be available in your day-to-day training environment and may be used to complement the requirements of the mandatory competencies. Professional development is recorded in the professional development record. Information recorded includes the date of the activity, the subject, the number of hours and the type of professional development (personal, technical or professional).

In the context of your career, your professional development never ends. When you have completed your professional development for APC purposes, RICS then requires you, as a member, to undertake lifelong learning, or continuing professional development (CPD) as it is sometimes known thereafter. The concept of professional development for the APC is explored in more detail in chapter 2.

Change of employer

If you change employer during the training period you should continue your records in the usual way, but there must be a clear note of the change of employer. In particular, the new position regarding your supervisor and/or counsellor must be indicated for the purposes of certification at the final assessment. RICS must also be advised of the change of employer using the 'change of employer form' available at www.rics.org/apc. RICS will record the change or detail the action you need to take to resolve any problems.

Important dates and deadlines – a chronology of the APC

Now that we have reviewed some of the key concepts and documents for the APC, we will take a brief look at some of the important dates and deadlines to which you will need to adhere during the training period.

Enrolment

A delay of a few weeks in your enrolment could put your final assessment back six months, as final assessments are normally held only twice a year. Closing dates are given on www.rics.org/apc where you will also find detailed support.

The enrolment form is available from the RICS Contact Centre. You must send the enrolment form, completed by yourself and your employer with the correct fee, to RICS Membership Operations. Details of the fees are included with the enrolment form. You must submit all the required material otherwise your enrolment cannot be accepted.

Once accepted, RICS will confirm your registration and give you a start date for recording your experience.

Acknowledgment by RICS

RICS will confirm your registration and give you a date from which you may start recording your experience. Don't forget the importance of this date, as before you reach the final assessment, if you are a graduate route 1 candidate, you will need to have completed a minimum of 400 days' experience within 23 calendar months (for a graduate route 2 candidate you will need to have completed 200 days experience within 11 months).

To be considered for either a session 1 or 2 assessment in a given year, you must have completed the required minimum training period. It follows, therefore, that a delay of a few weeks in enrolling could put the assessment date back by six months. You will need to decide your target final assessment date with your supervisor and counsellor. All the assessment information is available at www.rics.org/apc

Three-monthly reviews by your supervisor

Every three months your supervisor will discuss and review your progress against the competencies and you will complete the candidate achievement record and experience record.

Six-monthly reviews by your counsellor

At six-monthly intervals your counsellor will discuss and review your progress against the competencies and you will complete the candidate achievement record and experience record. Your counsellor's assessment constitutes a second opinion to that of the supervisor and will be completed in consultation with you and your supervisor.

Final assessment

It is your responsibility to keep all key dates in your work schedule. All the assessment information is available at www.rics.org/apc. You will have decided your target final assessment date with your supervisor and counsellor and you will need to send in the completed application form within the dates specified on www.rics.org. You will then have approximately one month to submit the required documents for the final assessment presentation and interview. Details of the required documents can be found on www.rics.org

Results

RICS will send your results by first class post 21 days after your interview. It is your responsibility to check

RICS has your up to date address. You will receive either a pass or a referral. If you are successful you will be awarded professional membership of RICS (MRICS). If you receive a referral you will be informed of the next steps to be taken.

For security and data protection reasons, RICS will not give results over the telephone, by fax, email or to a third party.

Appeals

An appeal, if appropriate, should be received by RICS no later than ten days from the date of your result letter. Details of how to make an appeal are on www.rics.org

When an appeal is made it must:

- be in writing, accompanied by the appropriate fee;

- be made by you and not a third party; and

- clearly state the grounds on which the appeal is being made, supported by appropriate evidence.

Finding help

Completing the APC carries with it a lot of responsibility and commitment. Both support and guidance are available for candidates and employers and for many queries you can contact RICS (see page 121).

There are also others who are there to help you and your employer with your APC, including:

- your employer, your supervisor and your counsellor;

- APC doctors;

- RICS regional training advisers (RTA); and

- other candidates (perhaps by way of the APC Discussion Forum).

Your employer, your supervisor and your counsellor

Now that we have considered the key concepts behind the APC you will see that this is not something you can do on your own. Your employer will play a critical role in your APC both in the context of providing you with the necessary structured training and in assessing your progress against the competencies.

It may be that you have been working for your employer for some time before starting the APC or you may be specifically seeking employment that will support you through this. Either way you may be considering how you can ensure that your employer will be able to provide you with the support you need. Some questions you should consider are:

- Is the employer listed on the RICS website as having an approved structured training agreement?

- Does the employer have a proven track record of training APC candidates? Does the employer have its own schemes for providing professional development?

- Does the employer have Investor in People accreditation? The Investor in People standard is given to firms who set high standards in terms of their commitment to, and their planning, delivery and evaluation of training and development for their staff.

- How does the employer plan to assist you in meeting the competency requirements? Can everything be done in-house? Will you be moved between departments or offices? Are secondments or exchanges available with other firms to make up any shortfalls? In addition, you might like to ask if you can speak to any of the firm's current or recent APC candidates.

- Who will be your supervisor and counsellor, and what is their experience of the APC?

Patience and understanding is also recommended. Most candidates have an expectation of being ready for the final assessment as soon as the minimum training period of 400 days within 23 calendar months (for graduate route 1) has elapsed. This is not always possible and sometimes, because of business practicalities or priorities, your employer may not have been able to give you the full spread of training against the competencies. Alternatively, you may not have progressed against certain competencies as quickly as expected. Don't forget, we all develop at different speeds in any of life's skills.

You should only apply for your final assessment when you, your supervisor and your counsellor feel you are ready and feel confident that you have gained the necessary training and experience – even if that means that your training period lasts for 30, or even 36, months. Be prepared to cooperate with your employer and, most importantly, listen to the advice of your supervisor and counsellor.

While you will develop certain expectations concerning your APC training, your employer will also be looking for a return from you by way of hard work, enterprise and fee income! You will need to approach the partnership with your employer with a degree of understanding and awareness, giving careful thought as to how you will balance the demands of your employer with your own need to make progress with the APC.

Finally, the importance of the employer cannot be overemphasised in terms of the appointment of your supervisor and counsellor, who, generally speaking, will be part of your employer's team. Your supervisor and counsellor will act as guides and mentors throughout and in a lot of instances beyond your training period and their roles will be of particular importance during preparation for your final assessment. It is important that this is an active partnership, where the employer takes a proactive approach, by way of interest and involvement, in your training and development.

It is sometimes said that it is only the large firms who can provide the best opportunities for APC training and that small firms may struggle. However, a small firm with a varied portfolio of work can provide more than adequate training and experience for APC candidates.

So, do not be slow in coming forward; it's in your own best interest to find an employer who will provide you with the training and experience you need to ensure that success at the final assessment interview is a formality. But do not lose sight of the fact that you are entering into a partnership and that your employer will also want a return on the investment.

RICS training advisers (RTAs)

RICS employs training advisers for each region in the UK. Details may be found on the RICS website at www.rics.org/apc

The role of the RTAs is to advise employers on all aspects of the APC. Most importantly, they help firms develop structured training agreements and provide approvals for these (see chapter 2 for more information). In drawing up such an agreement the RTA will provide advice to your employer. When your employer has prepared a training agreement that meets with the minimum standards, the RTA will confirm approval and it may then be used as an indicator of excellence and of the firm's commitment to APC training.

You should encourage your employer to discuss the structured training agreement and any APC training issues they may have with the local RTA.

APC doctors

Whereas the primary role of the RTAs is to support and advise employers, voluntary APC doctors are available to assist and guide candidates through the system. They are normally locally based and, where practical, will be from the same professional group as your own. They are often recently successful APC candidates and can therefore provide others with the benefit of their first-hand experience. Details of local APC doctors can be found on www.rics.org

Reading material

There is a wealth of reading material and information available from www.ricsbooks.com. You may find it particularly useful to use the RICS online knowledge resource for property professionals – *isurv* (www.isurv.com). The *isurv* 'channels' cover a huge range of surveying topics, mixing expert commentary with official RICS guidance. The *isurv* APC channel also holds excellent support material (www.isurv.com/apc).

Other candidates

Sharing ideas and approaches with other candidates can be an excellent way to find answers to queries and to gain advice. This might be through your local RICS Matrics group, through local events or perhaps by way of the APC Discussion Forum on the RICS website.

Summary

- It is essential to read the APC guidance available at www.rics.org/apc

- For graduate route 1 you will need to complete a minimum two-year period (400 days within a minimum of 23 calendar months) of training and practical experience.

- For graduate route 2 the minimum period is 200 days within 11 calendar months.

- It is important that you have a clear picture of what is meant by the term 'competent to practise', with regard to knowledge; problem-solving abilities; business and practice skills; personal and interpersonal skills; and the Rules of Conduct and professional ethics.

- A structured training agreement must be completed by your employer.

- Training and practical experience culminates in the final assessment: a one-hour interview with a panel of three (sometimes two) experienced practitioners, who will consider whether you are 'competent to practise'.

- Information and evidence of training and experience must be kept in your diary, candidate achievement record and experience record.

- You must undertake a minimum of 48 hours of professional development for every 12 months of training completed.

- If you change employer, you must notify RICS.

- RICS will give you a start date for recording your experience.

- All assessment information is available on www.rics.org/apc. You will have decided your target final assessment date with your supervisor.

- Results will be sent by first class post 21 days after your interview. If you are referred and wish to appeal, you must do so no later than 10 days from the date of your results letter.

- Help with the APC is available from RICS and APC doctors.

- Help for your employer is available from RTAs.

- Remember the APC is all about a partnership between yourself and your employer.

The training period

2

This chapter looks at how to go about managing your training period. It aims to develop your understanding of the competencies and illustrate how professional development can be used as a tool to assist your progress. Structured training will be considered in some detail, with particular regard to the various templates that need to be completed.

The competencies

A key aspect to the successful management of the training period is an in-depth knowledge and understanding of the competencies and requirements of each RICS professional group, which are contained in the appropriate APC pathway. Further guidance on the pathways is available at www.rics.org/apc

Chapter 1 discussed the meaning of the word 'competent' and explored what is meant by a competency. In the broader context, the use of competency-based training and, most importantly, competency-based interviewing, is fast becoming a worldwide phenomenon. As your career progresses and develops, you will find that your appreciation of this subject will grow. However, at this stage it is important that you fully understand competencies in the context of your APC. The advice that follows is therefore tailored to fit that particular need.

The APC guidance sets out what you need to achieve by way of skills and abilities over the training period. It indicates the specific competency requirements of each pathway, with guidelines on the number of competencies to be covered during the training period, and the depth and level of attainment required.

The competency choices must be made in consultation and with the agreement of your counsellor and supervisor and must reflect the work you carry out in your day-to-day environment. This choice will be considered as a reflection of your judgment at the final assessment. The APC guidance on each pathway will give a further insight into the experience requirements.

The APC guidance also sets out the full list of competencies in alphabetical order, with a reference for each – for example, Inspection TO44. This reference number is for use on your candidate achievement record and your experience record.

The competencies are varied and cover a wide range of technical, professional practice, business, management and interpersonal skills. For each competency, there are three levels of attainment:

- Level 1 – knowledge and understanding of the areas covered by the competency;

- Level 2 – application of this knowledge and understanding in normal practical situations; and

- Level 3 – ability to provide reasoned advice and depth of technical knowledge.

Consider the example below of the building surveying competency of 'building pathology', which progresses in complexity across the levels.

Building pathology

Level 1: demonstrate your knowledge and understanding of building defects including collection of information, measurements and tests.

Level 2: apply your knowledge to undertake surveys, use survey and other information to diagnose cause and mechanisms of failure.

Level 3: provide evidence of reasoned advice and appropriate recommendations, including the preparation and presentation of reports.

A typical final assessment question for this competency might be:

'I notice from your summaries of experience that you have carried out building surveys on a number of traditionally built 1960s houses. Describe how you went about those surveys [level 1]. What were the common types of failure to brickwork observed while carrying out those inspections? What were the causes and how did you diagnose these? [level 2]. What method of repair did you recommend to your client, and why? What sort of issues did you include in your final report and recommendations? [level 3].'

The guidance on pathways further illuminates the experience requirements within each of the competencies. Set out overleaf is an explanation of the experience required in the building pathology competency taken from the building surveying pathway guidance.

Building pathology

Level 1: Demonstrate knowledge and understanding of:

- typical defects relating to typical buildings found in your locality that you may have come across and explain cause and effect of these;
- building defects likely to be encountered in typical building surveying activities, e.g. wet and dry rot, flat roof defects, concrete defects, etc.;
- the various methods to collect, store and retrieve information for various differing purposes when carrying out property inspections;
- the various different types of inspection that may be carried out and the importance of accurate recording of information during inspection; and
- differing types of testing and the limitations of the tests, e.g. the use of damp meters and borescopes.

Level 2:

- explain in detail cause and mechanics of varying types of failure;
- explain procedures for carrying out inspections of properties;
- be able to explain, using detailed examples, the relationship between observations taken on site and the diagnosis of failure in building fabric;
- be able to use examples, from your own experience, to demonstrate your application of knowledge gained at level 1; and
- be able to use knowledge and information gathered from several sources, including if necessary specialist inspections to diagnose and explain building fabric failure.

> **Level 3:**
> - prepare reports for clients, explaining in non-technical language the causes of failure and the likely results of failure, together with the appropriate remedial measures;
> - using information gathered from inspections formulate the necessary remedial/preventative works including specific detail in the form of a schedule of works if required;
> - show an understanding of the level of detail required in typical reports, including examples of layout and the use of sketches, drawings and photographs;
> - be able to discuss in detail examples of unusual defects you have been involved with and remedial works employed; and
> - be able to demonstrate the differing requirements of reports to clients, e.g. the differences between schedules of condition, schedules of dilapidations and pre-acquisition reports.

You will reach these levels in a logical progression and in successive stages. There is no minimum number of days of training required to achieve a particular level of attainment in any of the competencies. In discussion with your supervisor and counsellor, a decision will be made as to when you have reached the required level of skill and ability in any particular competency. The number of days taken to reach the appropriate level will be dependent upon a combination of the following factors:

- your starting point – have you had any previous experience?;
- your aptitude and speed of learning in the competency;
- the quality of the training and experience given by the employer; and

- the particular competency – is it merely measurement, or nuclear physics?

For some candidates who already have experience prior to starting the APC some levels of competencies may be achieved from the outset. The judgment as to your achievement will be made by your supervisor and counsellor, who will then confirm this, and you will be able to update your candidate achievement record accordingly.

Each pathway requires you to satisfy three types of competency:

1 mandatory competencies;

2 core competencies; and

3 optional competencies.

The mandatory competencies generally relate to professional practice, interpersonal, management and business skills and are common to all pathways. The core competencies relate to the primary skills of your chosen pathway. The optional competencies are selected by you from a list contained in the APC guidance for the appropriate pathway.

The mandatory competencies – outline

The minimum standards for mandatory competencies are set out in the APC guidance and are structured in levels. You must achieve the minimum standards, as follows:

• Conduct rules, ethics and professional practice	To Level 3
• Client care • Communication and negotiation • Health and safety	To Level 2

• Accounting principles and procedures • Business planning • Conflict avoidance, management and dispute resolution procedures • Data management • Sustainability • Teamworking	To Level 1

All of the above competencies are defined in the APC guidance.

In addition, candidates following the senior professional route must achieve the following three competencies:

• leadership (to level 2);

• managing people (to level 2);

• managing resources (to level 2).

The minimum standards described above may also be included at a higher level, if appropriate to the particular pathway. If a pathway includes a mandatory competency to a higher level, this will also appear in the core or optional competency list for that pathway, to the higher level.

Overall, when your employer develops your structured training agreement, they will need to set out how you will achieve the required mandatory, core and optional competencies. Your employer will identify the mandatory competencies where you will receive the appropriate training within your day-to-day work, as part of your structured training. This will leave you with a remainder which may require you to undertake additional learning or experience or a specific training course. These actions may qualify for your professional development.

The mandatory competencies – in detail

The mandatory competencies are one of the most important parts of the whole APC. The skills and abilities they encourage and test underpin all professional and technical aspects of working as a surveyor, and are vital for further advancement in the profession.

This chapter will do two things: first, give some further explanation of the requirements for each competency; and second, provide some practical advice on how to help you achieve the required levels, working through the levels outlined.

The advice is not intended to be all-encompassing, or definitive in any way – each candidate, each pathway, and each firm will alter the ingredients of each competency slightly. It is certainly not possible to say, 'follow this, and you will pass'. What follows are simply suggestions and pointers as to how the requirements of the competencies might be met.

In particular, you should note that the recommended reading is not exhaustive – it is, in the main, a selection of some good texts. Each pathway will have its own specialist authors and texts, and you should talk to your supervisor and counsellor, asking for their views and recommendations based on their experience, which should be more tailored to your pathway.

Some of the training suggested for the mandatory competencies – particularly the structured reading – may also prove useful for professional development purposes. Remember that some 32 hours of professional development a year must be focused around the areas of the mandatory competencies (16 hours on mandatory competencies and a further 16 hours on professional practice). In particular, you may wish to use the RICS online knowledge resource for property professionals – *isurv* (www.isurv.com). This service, mixing expert commentary with official RICS guidance, covers a huge range of surveying matters, and can be used for professional development purposes.

The minimum requirements for the competencies in the mandatory competency list vary from level 1 to level 3. Where a competency is required to a level higher than 1, I will explain how to move from one level to the next. Remember it is important to achieve the required levels in a progressive manner. You cannot just achieve level 3 from a standing start so it is important that you understand the requirements at each level.

For each of the competencies discussed you should refer to the APC guidance for the detailed definitions. The following sections simply provide further practical guidance to support these definitions.

Conduct rules, ethics and professional practice

This competency must be achieved at level 3.

Level I

The knowledge and understanding required of the candidate at level 1 is wide-ranging. It covers the role, function and significance of RICS; an understanding of society's expectations of professional practice; RICS Rules of Conduct for both firms and members; and the general principles of law and the legal system, as applicable in your area of practice

The RICS Rules of Conduct, policies and associated help sheets are available on www.rics.org. You should make sure that you are aware of the Rules for both members and firms.

To understand the role and function of RICS, you should carry out some reading around the structure of RICS, the various professional groups, group boards and committees, and the functions performed, such as advising the government on housing, taxation, planning and landlord and tenant issues and bringing an influence to bear on all relevant aspects of society. Apart from keeping abreast of developments in newspapers, a good source of information is the RICS magazine, *RICS Business*, and the various other RICS and 'property' publications.

The other requirement at level 1 involves the candidate understanding the role of the professional person and of society's expectations of such a person. The general principles of professional integrity (the twelve standards listed below) hold good in all professional-client situations. An important issue is that of 'ethics', which have been defined as a set of moral principles extending beyond a formal code of conduct.

RICS expects members to act both within the Rules of Conduct and to maintain professional and ethical standards. Members are expected to apply a set of twelve standards in order to meet the high standards of behaviour expected of them. These standards are to:

- Act honourably;

- Act with integrity;

- Be open and transparent in your dealings;

- Be accountable for all your actions;

- Know and act within your limitations;

- Be objective at all times;

- Always treat others with respect;

- Set a good example;

- Have the courage to make a stand;

- Comply with relevant laws and regulations;

- Avoid conflicts of interest; and

- Respect confidentiality.

Level 2

Level 2 in this competency requires you to provide evidence of practical application in your area of practice, being able to justify actions at all times and demonstrate personal commitment to the Rules of Conduct, ethics and the twelve standards.

Level 3

At level 3, you should be able to provide evidence of the application of the above in your area of practice in the context of advising clients.

Practical guidance

This particular mandatory competency is a huge and expansive topic – but it should be kept in perspective. The final assessment panel will keep their testing and questioning within the confines of the knowledge and experience that a person with two years experience in the surveying industry, and occupying a fairly junior position, will have gained. Therefore you will not be expected to have first-hand experience of some of the more detailed areas of the Rules of Conduct, such as your firm's professional indemnity insurance or the Members' Accounts Regulations, but you will be expected to demonstrate your knowledge of the requirements of RICS in these areas and how this would be implemented in practice.

The assessment panel may also test your knowledge around some of the basics, such as why RICS has Rules of Conduct, and aspects of the twelve standards.

Your training should incorporate a mixture of practical experience, structured reading and perhaps some CPD-type events on current issues. This competency is obviously also an ideal subject for your professional development. The APC guidance recommends that training in this area accounts for 16 of the 48 hours per year of professional development experience required.

A useful source of information is the APC guidance on the Rules of Conduct, RICS *guidance note for APC/ATC candidates, supervisors and counsellors: Rules of Conduct*, available from www.rics.org/apc

Levels 2 and 3 will involve you developing your practical experience at work, with an emphasis on taking instructions, understanding and dealing with conflicts of interest, and applying the rules and the twelve standards.

At your three-monthly and six-monthly reviews, you can discuss this with your supervisor and counsellor. You may wish to consider three main areas:

- *the role and function of RICS*: 'What have you read about RICS activities in recent months?'

- *the twelve standards*: 'Give me an example of a time at which you have had to know and act within your limitations?'; 'Tell me about an occasion when you had to have the courage to make a stand?'

- *Rules of Conduct*: 'What have you read this quarter ... and what do you understand about the Rules of Conduct concerning client accounts/or similar?'

Some examples of questions asked by assessment panels for this competency are:

- If you are successful with your APC and you decide to start your own business as a chartered surveyor what sort of things will you need to consider and do? For this question, assessors are looking for the candidate to demonstrate that they will:

  - meet the requirements of the code;

  - understand the need for insurances (employers liability, public liability, etc.), a health and safety policy, equal opportunities policy, etc.; and

29

- use the RICS logo as set out by RICS and use only the appropriate alternative designation relevant to their professional group.

• What is client's money and how can a firm preserve the security of this?

• If you are approched in respect of an instruction and agree terms over the telephone what would you then need to do and what details would you need to provide?

• If you are successful in undertaking a project for a client and they send you a case of wine as a thank you, what should you do?

• You are working for a surveying practice and a friend asks you to ... [example of work from the relevant professional group] ... as a favour because you are a surveyor, what should you do?

You will see from the above examples how the questions tend to be scenario based and will often take a candidate into areas in which they may not have direct experience.

The RICS Regulation website (www.rics.org/newregulation) provides an excellent source of information regarding the RICS Rules of Conduct, including details of disciplinary hearings and minutes of the meetings of the Regulatory Board.

Finally, you should of course ensure that you provide evidence of this competency in your experience record and professional development record – give examples of structured reading and training and also of practical experience and make sure that all your detailed activities clearly comply with the Rules of Conduct and associated standards.

For further information and guidance on the RICS Rules of Conduct the DVD *RICS Rules of Conduct* available from RICS Books is a very useful resource. The DVD is designed to inform and challenge your knowledge and raise awareness of the depth and the breadth of the Rules of Conduct and what is expected of a professional.

Client care

This competency is required to be achieved to level 2. At level 1, you should be able to demonstrate a knowledge and understanding of the principle and practice of client care, including:

- the concept of identifying clients, colleagues and third parties who are your clients and understand the behaviours that are appropriate to establish good client relationships;

- the systems and procedures that are appropriate for managing the process of client care including complaints; and

- the requirements to collect data, analyse and define the needs of clients.

At level 2, you should be able to apply all of the above in your area of business or practice on a routine basis.

Practical guidance

Approaches to client care will vary from business to business, depending on the nature of the work, the degree of client interface and the type of organisation. At one extreme – residential valuation, sales and letting – there is a high degree of customer interface, and the skill of managing and influencing clients is vital, with the business relying solely on fee income for survival. In areas of central or local government, by contrast, the link is not so direct and the dependency on fee income from transactions not as great.

However, one key concept is fundamental to all business: the client is sovereign. Notice that this is not the same as saying, 'the customer is always right' – in surveying matters this is not always the case! You must be able to understand the link between customer care and duty of care.

If a client wishes to do something that would be impractical, or impossible, or doomed to certain failure, the surveyor owes the client a duty of care to inform him or her of that. To give the best customer care, you must therefore have a good understanding of each client's needs.

This is one of those competencies where you must be able to 'step back' out of a situation, to analyse what it is that you have learnt about customer care and duty of care in any particular instance. In preparation for the final assessment you should be able to explain a situation in which you have delivered good client care in the context of your work. You should discuss with your supervisor and counsellor opportunities where you can develop skills in this area.

To assist your understanding of this subject, you may also wish to undertake some structured reading and training.

This competency is very closely related to professional practice and ethics.

Communication and negotiation

This competency is required to be achieved at level 2. At level 1, you are required to demonstrate a knowledge and understanding of effective oral, written, graphic and presentation skills, including methods and techniques appropriate to specific situations. At level 2, you are required to provide evidence of practical application of oral, written, graphic and presentation skills that are appropriate in a variety of situations, specifically where negotiation is involved.

Practical guidance – communication skills

Oral communication is used in a wide range of surveying situations and circumstances: at meetings, in negotiations, when managing people, when making presentations, in tenders, and so on. In my experience, there is some basic best practice for all situations. This can then be tailored to meet the requirements of specific situations. The list of specific situations is of course huge, and training will also be wide and varied.

Communication skills can be improved by additional training. Many organisations run courses in this area – these may include, for example, assertiveness training courses. However, for most candidates, the best approach is to be coached by senior people in your particular area, and to put your developing skills continually into practice.

On a general level, any course or training programme should cover the nature and purposes of oral communication – addressing the different approaches to be taken in different situations, and the techniques that can be used to communicate effectively.

In addition, there are many texts on the subject, allowing training to be complemented by structured reading. A search on the RICS Books website (www.ricsbooks.com) for 'communication skills' will identify a number of excellent publications.

Of course the final assessment interview includes a ten-minute presentation as well as communication via questioning and this, therefore, gives an excellent opportunity for the panel to assess this competency.

Written and graphic communication will cover a wide range of situations and encompass a variety of skills. It will include the use of emails, letters and reports, for all of which an essential component is being able to write good, unambiguous prose.

For level 1, you must be able to understand the various media in which written communications can be presented, and more importantly, the skills involved in doing so, with regard to the target audience, the length, style and layout of the communication, the message you wish to convey, and the structure of the communication. In terms of 'graphic' communication, it covers sketch notes, drawings in plans, designs linked to the construction process and similar (if these are relevant to your chosen pathway).

It is probably easiest to assess understanding with reference to actual written work – your own and other people's – in a variety of mediums. Consider why a particular communication fails or succeeds, how it could be improved, and what the aspects are that make it successful in a particular area.

For level 2, put this knowledge into practice. Consider a range of your written work, in a variety of media. Is it all appropriate for the audience and purpose? Have you achieved, in a letter, report, email, sketch or design what you set out to achieve?

If you are experiencing difficulties in this area, you could attend a course (internal or external) on written communication. There are also a lot of useful books and texts on the subject, again available through RICS Books. Nobody would expect you to write a perfect client report the first time you tried, but with a full understanding of the principles and purposes of the report, and some more practice, you will be much better equipped to do so.

The critical analysis submitted by you for the final assessment provides an easy opportunity for the panel to assess your ability in this area.

Practical guidance – negotiation skills

This competency overlaps somewhat with the 'conflict avoidance' competency (see page 38).

To fulfil the requirements of this particular competency, check that you understand what lies behind successful negotiations: the preparation of evidence; an understanding of the various approaches to negotiations; a knowledge of where and how parameters are set; a knowledge of what each side wishes to get from the negotiations, and from any future relationship; and so on.

If possible, ask your supervisor and counsellor to involve you in negotiations carried out by your firm. This is perhaps the best way of helping you to gain an understanding of the principles and skills.

Health and safety

The basic level 1 requirement of this competency is to demonstrate a knowledge and understanding of the principles and responsibilities with regard to health and safety imposed by law and codes of practice and other regulations relating to health and safety appropriate to your area of practice.

This competency must be taken to level 2 where you will be required to provide evidence of practical application of health and safety issues and the requirements for compliance, in your area of practice.

Practical guidance

This competency covers all aspects of a surveyor's working life. It is about ensuring that the surveyor's entire working life is conducted as safely as possible with as little risk to health as possible, and that the same is true for all of those around the surveyor.

It is easy to think of ways in which health and safety issues relate to, say, work on a construction site, but perhaps less so for more office-based work. However, the same basic philosophies underpin all work carried out in any environment. In off-site jobs, the issues encompass such things as your managers knowing where you are and what you are doing at all times, and, should you leave the office, when you will return and who you are meeting. There are also numerous health and safety issues relating to the use of equipment, in offices as well as all other locations, and on keeping employees healthy and safe.

Owing to the importance of health and safety, most firms and organisations conduct formal training and instruction on the relevant issues. Ensure that you attend this and that you can explain the reasons behind any requirements imposed by the firm.

The Health and Safety Executive (HSE) provides numerous free leaflets on its website, at www.hse.gov.uk, including lists of its current publications. You should visit the site and select some useful reading.

Finally, you must be able to demonstrate knowledge of the health and safety legislation and codes of practice that apply to your area of work and also evidence of practical application as required by level 2 of the competency. This will differ from one pathway to another, but includes such things as the *Health and Safety at Work Act* 1974, the *Construction (Design and Management) Regulations* 2007 and the *Control of Asbestos Regulations* 2006. You must be aware of relevant legislation and be able to explain it and its significance to your area of work.

Accounting principles and procedures

This competency must be achieved to level 1. The requirement is to demonstrate knowledge and understanding of fundamental accounting concepts plus the format and preparation of management and company accounts, including profit and loss statements, cash flow statements and balance sheets.

Practical guidance

You will undoubtedly be able to gain some experience – practical or theoretical – of these concepts in the course of your work. If there is one particular aspect that is unlikely to arise in your everyday work, consider how your training might be arranged so that this is covered.

You may also like to read a textbook on the subject, or attend an appropriate training course or CPD lecture.

It should be noted that some candidates might quite easily reach levels 2 and 3 in this competency, if this subject is part of your job. For example, a rural practice candidate working for an estate would deal with these types of issues regularly. Candidates working in commercial property and dealing, perhaps, with the leisure and entertainments industry, might also easily attain level 2 or 3 through practical experience, particularly where accounts are used for valuation purposes.

Business planning

This competency must be achieved to level 1. The requirement is to demonstrate knowledge and understanding of how business management activities contribute to the achievement of corporate objectives.

Practical guidance

This is a vast subject, and most candidates generally benefit by attending some kind of basic management training course, where possible. These are run by a number of bodies, including Open University and the Chartered Management Institute. Many employers also offer training in this area. You may well not be directly involved in managing your business, and this is not expected of you for the purposes of level 1, but you must be able to understand – and explain to the assessors, if necessary – the underlying factors of business management.

A lot will also be learned on the job, of course, and coaching and training from an experienced supervisor or counsellor will be invaluable. There is a lot of overlap with the requirements of the other mandatory competencies (communications and negotiation, teamworking, client care, and so on). Reading a management skills textbook will also develop knowledge and understanding of issues such as motivation, mission statements, strategy, organisational structures, and so on.

A useful textbook in this respect is *The handbook of management and leadership: a guide to managing for results* by Michael Armstrong and Tina Stephens (Kogan Page, London, 2005). This book covers the practice of management, delivering change, enhancing customer relations and enabling continuous improvement.

Conflict avoidance, management and dispute resolution procedures

This competency must be achieved to level 1. This requires knowledge and understanding of the techniques for conflict avoidance, conflict management and dispute resolution procedures, including for example adjudication and arbitration appropriate to your APC pathway.

Practical guidance

The 'ingredients' of this competency will vary greatly between the various pathways. In commercial practice, for example, landlord and tenant matters will be fairly common, while in construction, this competency will be present everyday in managing building contracts. Indeed, in the construction pathway (Quantity surveying and Construction), this becomes a core competency to level 2, with requirements based around procurement and the drafting of terms and conditions of leases, contracts and agreements.

In basic terms, and across all pathways, it is important that you understand how to conduct negotiations, and also the various options available should negotiations break down, working through mediation and conciliation, adjudication, arbitration, independent expert determination, and, finally, litigation.

You may be encouraged to sit in on negotiations at your firm from an early stage in your career. Also you will benefit from some formal training on this and other aspects of dispute resolution, covering the preparation of evidence, case law, approaches and tactics. It is reasonably likely that by the time you reach the final assessment, you will have had practical experience of running your own negotiations, or participating in other dispute resolution procedures, and will thus be able to discuss this. As part of your training plan ensure that you make steady progress towards this end.

There are also many texts available on this subject. To get started, the following RICS guidance notes and practice statements are useful documents:

- *Surveyors acting as arbitrators and as independent experts in commercial property rent reviews*;

- *Surveyors acting as adjudicators in the construction industry*;

- *Surveyors acting as expert witnesses*; and

- *Surveyors acting as advocates*.

All of these publications are available in hardcopy from RICS Books (www.ricsbooks.com). RICS members can download the publications as a PDF from www.rics.org

In addition, don't forget CPD-type lectures or training that may be available within your firm, or from external providers.

Data management

This competency must be achieved to level 1. It involves demonstrating knowledge and understanding of the sources of information and data applicable to your area of practice, including the methodologies and techniques most appropriate to collect, collate and store data.

Practical guidance

Again, this competency will vary greatly between the APC pathways. It is important to think of it in relation to your specific route, and against the backdrop of your day-to-day work and the particular IT developments in your area.

In the valuation pathway, for example, this competency will cover comparable evidence found in sales and rental evidence. Collection, collation and storage methods in this pathway will usually comprise the use of IT spreadsheets and databases, either developed by firms or sold as commercial packages. Developments in this area, and in the commercial property pathway, include the use of computer assisted techniques.

In the quantity surveying and construction pathway, meanwhile, sources of data may be previous contracts or cost guides and price books. Various commercial packages are also available to price contracts and bills of quantities.

For all pathways, the important thing is for you to be able to understand the use of data in your day-to-day work – how this is gathered and put to use, and what the best methods of collection, collation and storage are. You should be able to step back mentally from your work, to explain what data you use, how you find it and how it is manipulated. You should also be aware of the implications of data protection legislation and how this will affect the use that can be made of data you may hold.

You should avoid the temptation to 'write this competency off', on the basis that it will be covered at level 1 elsewhere – for example, in level 1 of the valuation competency. Try to use the competency to broaden and develop your understanding of wider data issues and developments in the profession. See this competency as a subject in itself and carry out some structured reading. Discuss it as a discrete issue at some point in your training plan and at the three- and six-monthly review stages.

Sustainability

As a mandatory competency this is required to level 1. It requires a knowledge and understanding of why and how sustainability seeks to balance economic, environmental and social objectives at local, national and global levels, in the context of land, property and the built environment.

Practical guidance

All chartered surveyors need a basic understanding of environmental issues, which range from groundwater pollution and contaminated land, to control of pollution in the air we breathe, as well as, very importantly, energy and climate change. Environmental issues affect building design, construction use and management, development and re-development, and regeneration and town planning. Issues such as global warming, dwindling national resources and atmospheric pollutants are top priorities with many government and influential bodies, such as the EU and the World Trade Organisation (WTO).

You should carry out some general reading in newspapers and professional journals on environmental issues. Other useful sources of information and advice are the RICS guidance notes:

- *Contamination and environmental issues – their implications for property professionals*;

- *Sustainability and the RICS property lifecyle*; and

- *Carbon management of real estate.*

Surveying Sustainability: a short guide for the property professional, produced in partnership between RICS, Forum for the Future and Gleeds is also useful.

In addition, of course, you should maintain an awareness of environmental issues whilst at work. You should be aware of any government initiatives, laws or EU regulations affecting your particular area of work. The Department of Energy and Climate Change (DECC) website is a useful resource (www.decc.gov.uk). On a more local level, be aware of any internal office environmental policies (recycling of paper, for example), and be able to explain the purposes of these. You may like to test your knowledge and understanding in this area by considering how you would express the firm's 'green credentials', should this be requested, for example, in an invitation to tender. Once more, this is a case of stepping back from day-to-day work, to consider the environmental factors that underlie and overarch such work.

Teamworking

This competency is required to level 1. Candidates must demonstrate knowledge and understanding of the principles, behaviour and dynamics of teamworking.

Practical guidance

This competency involves understanding why people work in teams, and some of the basic principles underlying teamworking. In practice, you will rarely not work within a team, so in effect, while the mandatory requirement is to level 1, in practice you will often be working to level 2 ('working as a team member in a work or business environment').

Evidence of working in a team will be easy to come by; however, the level 1 requirement is to *understand the principles* behind this. You should therefore consider a situation in which you have witnessed or experienced teamworking, and be able to explain how that team worked, concentrating on the roles each member adopted and the success or otherwise of this.

Your understanding can be complemented and extended by some reading on the subject. A leading text on this subject is *Management teams: Why they succeed or fail* by R. M. Belbin (Butterworth-Heinemann, Oxford, 2003).

A last word of advice

Hopefully you now have a better idea of what the mandatory competencies entail, and of how to achieve them. Remember that the philosophies behind the mandatory competencies, and the business skills inherent in them, will be encountered in every aspect of your working life. It is for this reason that they are mandatory!

The above only deals with the competencies in relation
to the training period. We will return to the competencies
when we look at the final assessment interview in
chapter 5; for now, simply note that the final assessment
interview is a largely competency-based interview,
although some questions may relate to matters of a more
general nature.

Professional development

For each 12 months of practical training that is
completed, you must undertake an annual minimum of
48 hours of professional development. If you are
studying for your RICS accredited degree by part time
study or distance learning whilst undertaking your APC
structured training period then the final year of your
study can be used towards your professional
development for that year. You should however
undertake additional professional development to
supplement this.

The idea behind professional development is that it gives
you the opportunity to acquire some of the additional
skills and knowledge that it will not always be possible
for your employer to provide within the week-to-week
business of the practice. The APC guidance recommends
that you undertake 16 hours per year of professional
development in:

- personal skills development linked to mandatory
  competencies;

- technical skills development linked to your core and
  optional competencies; and

- professional practice skills development linked to
  professional practice competencies, code of conduct
  and conflicts of interest.

When you record your professional development activity in your professional development record you will be asked to allocate each activity to one of the above categories.

The professional development record template is shown in figure 2.

 RICS

Candidate Name - 1234567
Template 4
Select a Route

Professional Development Record

Commercial Property

Please detail the PD / LLL development title, location and key components. Include Method of Learning. Include an overview of the objective and reasoning why you are doing this PD / LLL development. Conclude with the outcome and how it relates to your declared competencies.

Year 1			
Date	**Subject** (objective, reasoning and outcome)	**Hours**	**PD Split?**
dd/mm/yyyy		0.0	Select a Split
dd/mm/yyyy		0.0	Select a Split
dd/mm/yyyy		0.0	Select a Split
dd/mm/yyyy		0.0	Select a Split
dd/mm/yyyy		0.0	Select a Split
dd/mm/yyyy		0.0	Select a Split
dd/mm/yyyy		0.0	Select a Split
dd/mm/yyyy		0.0	Select a Split
dd/mm/yyyy		0.0	Select a Split
dd/mm/yyyy		0.0	Select a Split
dd/mm/yyyy		0.0	Select a Split
dd/mm/yyyy		0.0	Select a Split
dd/mm/yyyy		0.0	Select a Split
dd/mm/yyyy		0.0	Select a Split
dd/mm/yyyy		0.0	Select a Split
dd/mm/yyyy		0.0	Select a Split
dd/mm/yyyy		0.0	Select a Split
		0.0	**Total**

Note: 96 hours in total required for Final Assessment (minimum 48 hours per year)

Hours	Total / Split
0.0	Personal
0.0	Technical
0.0	Professional

Figure 2 Professional development record

An important aspect of your professional development is that it should be planned and structured in such a way as to remain flexible. It should be designed to complement and support your training and development in the context of the various competencies. Professional development may comprise formal training courses or more informal types of learning, such as structured reading, distance-learning or e-learning programmes and secondments. It is important that you accept ownership of your professional development, recognising that the planning, acquiring and evaluating of it is your responsibility. Note that the APC guidance also provides excellent advice on professional development and in particular the principles which underpin professional development, such as it should:

- be gained in a structured manner;

- be based on an explicit process of selecting, planning and evaluating the activities; and

- reflect learning from informal training sources such as structured reading and secondments.

On a practical note, make sure that your professional development complements your structured training agreement, and ensure that you can provide evidence of a planned and systematic approach. There should be a clearly defined relationship between the topics selected and the competencies. If you feel that there is a need for variation regarding the number of hours allocated, discuss this with your supervisor and counsellor.

Structured training

In the context of the APC, this is training that is discussed, planned, reviewed and, if necessary, revised, and which, most importantly, forms the basis of an agreement between the parties.

The development of a structured training agreement is mandatory for all candidates and is prepared by your employer. It must be approved by your RICS training advisor and once approved your employer will be listed as holding an RICS approved structured training agreement on www.rics.org

Structured training agreement

A structured training agreement is a formal statement of your employer's commitment to the APC. It will also set out what you can expect from your employer and when.

It allows your employer to confirm to RICS that they have the will, the means and the intention of getting people qualified in accordance with the APC guidance and requirements.

Advice concerning the preparation of a structured training agreement can be found at www.rics.org/apc and in the APC guidance. You will find that most employers who have recently trained APC candidates will already have an approved training agreement in place and will be familiar with RICS requirements. Once an RICS training adviser has approved an organisation's structured training agreement this can be adapted for all candidates (although this assumes that the approved agreement covers your office location and your pathway, if not a new agreement may be needed). A training programme will then be tailored to suit you and your proposed training, in relation to timescales and competencies.

If a structured training agreement is not in place or a new agreement is needed, the guidance at www.rics.org/apc will provide a useful discussion document for you and your employer when planning and agreeing your training for the next two years. There is also a template available for download from www.rics.org/apc for use by your employer when developing a structured training agreement. Your employer may also invite an RICS training adviser to come in to talk through the requirements for structured training.

The structured training agreement template provides guidance only – your employer may wish to tailor an agreement more suited to his or her firm. The following information should generally be included within a structured training agreement:

- statements of commitment by your employer;

- information on the organisation and areas of activity;

- information on the organisation's policies regarding training and the APC, including how the professional development requirement will be met and supported; and

- a commitment to preparing a training programme for each candidate, including arrangements and timescales for monitoring the training programme.

Your training programme should comprise:

- a competency achievement planner setting out your chosen competencies and the timescales within which your supervisor and counsellor hope you will achieve each level of each competency; and

- a monitoring table (or similar) setting out the experience that will be available for each level of each competency that you need to achieve.

Summary

- Competencies are written to three levels and are generally progressive in terms of skills and abilities.

- There is no minimum requirement for the number of days needed to achieve each competency. The level of attainment is decided by your supervisor and counsellor in discussion with yourself.

- Mandatory competencies are compulsory for all candidates.

- Professional development should be linked to and used to complement your experience and linked to your competencies. At the final assessment your documentation must show evidence of a planned and systematic approach to professional development.

- Structured training is training that is discussed, planned and reviewed between the parties to the agreement. RICS training advisers (RTAs) can provide your employer with advice and support to help with developing a structured training agreement.

- An organisation's overall structured training agreement must be approved by an RTA (this is not required for each and every candidate once an approval has been given).

Information management

3

This chapter looks at the various records that you need to keep during the training period. It provides advice and guidance on how to keep these records and considers their importance in the context of the final assessment. The role of the supervisor and counsellor is also covered.

Why keep records?

You should be aware of the importance of the various records you need to keep in the context of both your continuous training and the final assessment. The information contained in your candidate achievement record, professional development record and experience record will not only provide the assessment panel with the evidence that you have met the minimum training requirements, but will also give a focus for lines of questioning during the final assessment interview. It is therefore vital that you manage and record this information during the training period in an organised and systematic manner, as this will greatly assist you in the final interview.

The records

Most of the records you need to keep have been considered briefly in outline in the previous chapters. The following guidance brings all of this together and provides some practical tips and advice.

Diary

A diary must be kept by all candidates. This is simply a day-to-day record of your training and experience.

Week: ....

Date	Nature of professional work carried out	Competency reference

Figure 3 Diary template

The diary will provide the information and detail that you will need to summarise in your experience record. It is also a very useful document to use to remind your supervisor and your counsellor of the detail of the work with which you have been involved between each of their assessments.

Your diary is not submitted as part of the final assessment documentation. However, it should always be kept up to date and be available for inspection by your RICS training adviser (RTA) on an office visit or by the final assessment panel, if requested. You can start recording experience after you have received confirmation of your enrolment (RICS will allow you to back date your experience for up to a month provided you have been employed by your current employer for that time – contact the Membership Operations department for more detail). The date shown in the acknowledgment of enrolment from RICS should, therefore, be the first entry in your diary. Remember that if you change employer, this must be clearly marked, with perhaps a couple of parallel lines to show a break and a few words of explanation . You must also advise RICS of this change by completing and returning the change of employer form available from www.rics.org/apc

There are five important pieces of advice regarding your diary:

1   Keep it up to date: do not let the weeks slip by without completion. Get into the habit of writing it on a weekly basis.

2   Only record experience in the core and optional competency areas, not the mandatory.

3   Record your experience in periods of no less than half a day (this may involve some 'packaging' of experience that has taken place over the week – so long as the balance of experience over the week in total is accurate, this is fine).

4   Get into the habit of using descriptions that relate to the various competencies, so that you can make easy links to your experience and candidate achievement records and to the competency achievement planner in your structured training agreement. For example, 'negotiation and agreement of repair works under a final schedule of dilapidations' will give you all of the links and reminders you need to properly complete your other documentation. It will also help when your supervisor and counsellor are reviewing your overall performance against your competency achievement planner.

5   You should use your diary as part of the preparation process for the final assessment. It is therefore important that it is well written and clearly presented, to help you when you are reviewing your training and experience over the two-year period, in preparation for the final assessment interview.

Candidate achievement record

The candidate achievement record includes your log book and your log book summary.

Your log book is a summary of the number of days of work experience recorded in your diary, for each competency, for each month of the training period.

		Months												
		1	2	3	4	5	6	7	8	9	10	11	12	Total
Number and Competency Title		Month Year	Month Year	Month Year	Month Year	Month Year	Month Year	Month Year	Month Year	Month Year	Month Year	Month Year	Month Year	Days
Technical - Core Competencies														
Technical - Optional Competencies														
Technical - Plus Competencies														
	Total													

Log Book - Year 1   Commercial Property   Candidate Name - 1234567   Template 3

Figure 4 Format for the log book

Get into the discipline of completing your log book at the end of each month. The log book is a very useful tool for the assessment panel. It provides an immediate snapshot of your areas of work experience and will be used, in conjunction with your experience record, to structure the final assessment interview to reflect your experience and your competency achievements.

You should complete your log book summary after each of your supervisor's and counsellor's assessments to reflect the competency achievements that have been confirmed by your supervisor or your counsellor at that time.

Professional development

Be proactive in recording your professional development. As explained in chapter 2, there are many aspects of your daily work that count as professional development, such as attending meetings, preparing to run a meeting or give a talk, structured reading, and so on. Make sure that you are fully aware of what constitutes professional development, and for further information take a look at www.rics.org. Keep a regular record in your diary – this record can then be transferred on a monthly basis to your professional development record. Do make sure that when you record time for professional development you do not also allocate this time as work experience. It can only be one or the other!

Experience record

The experience record is a record of your experience and training against your competencies. You should complete this record before each of your supervisor and counsellor assessments, using the document to summarise your diary for each of the competencies where you have gained further experience in that period. In total, for each level, once achieved you should aim to have written up to 200 words. Use the record to clearly demonstrate the projects and work with which you have been involved and show how these are linked to the relevant competencies. You should ideally name real life projects but if confidentiality is an issue then you should simply explain the type of project. Unlike the diary, you do need to discuss the mandatory competencies in your experience record so it may be useful to keep a separate note of experience in these areas to inform your experience record. Figure 5 opposite shows the experience record template for the commercial property pathway.

You should aim to make the experience record the focal point of your meetings with your supervisor at three-monthly intervals and with your counsellor at six-monthly intervals. You need to be proactive in managing your progress. Therefore, prepare this record in advance of these meetings, in order that it can be used by your supervisor and counsellor in assessing your progress.

Experience Record

Commercial Property

Please record your summary of experience / training completed against your declared competencies. **Note: Record against ALL declared Levels up to a maximum of 1000 characters per cell (approximately 150 to 200 words per Level)**. (PD / LLL should be recorded in Template 4).

Competency & level	Competency experience details	Job title / Employer
Mandatory Competencies		
M001 Accounting principles and procedures		
Level 1		
M002 Business planning		
Level 1		
M003 Client care		
Level 1		
Level 2		
M004 Communication and negotiation		
Level 1		
Level 2		
M005 Conduct rules, ethics and professional practice		
Level 1		
Level 2		
Level 3		
M006 Conflict avoidance, management and dispute resolution procedures		
Level 1		
M007 Data management		
Level 1		
M008 Health and safety		
Level 1		
Level 2		
M009 Sustainability		
Level 1		
M010 Teamworking		
Level 1		

Competency & level	Competency experience details	Job title / Employer
Technical - Core Competencies		
T044 Inspection		
Level 1		
Level 2		
Level 3		
T057 Measurement of land and property		
Level 1		
Level 2		
Level 3		
T083 Valuation		
Level 1		
Level 2		
Level 3		
Technical - Optional Competencies		
Select From Dropdown List		
Level 1		
Level 2		
Level 3		
Select From Dropdown List		
Level 1		
Level 2		
Level 3		
Select From Dropdown List		
Level 1		
Level 2		
Level 3		

Competency & level	Competency experience details	Job title / Employer
Technical - Optional PLUS Competencies		
Select From Dropdown List		
Level 1		
Level 2		
Level 3		
Select From Dropdown List		
Level 1		
Level 2		
Level 3		

Figure 5 Experience record template

Progress reports

The role of your supervisor and counsellor throughout the training period is most important. Detailed guidance

55

on these roles and responsibilities is available at www.rics.org/apc. There are, however, a few key issues worth noting:

- the supervisor is responsible for overseeing your day-to-day work, whereas the counsellor is responsible for managing your training at a strategic level;

- ideally, the supervisor and counsellor should be different people. However, the roles may be combined if, for instance, you are employed by a sole practitioner or if there are other reasons why it is appropriate that they are one and the same person;

- ideally, both parties should be chartered surveyors. However, the supervisor need not necessarily be a chartered surveyor. The counsellor must be a chartered surveyor;

- the supervisor should give guidance, support and encouragement on a regular basis and will usually be your line manager. At three-monthly intervals, he or she will assess your progress against the competencies and complete your progress reports;

- the counsellor has a similar but more strategic role, and will formally assess your progress on a six-monthly basis and complete the appropriate progress report. In reviewing your overall progress, the counsellor will provide a second opinion to that of the supervisor. The counsellor will also consider any adjustments that may be needed to your training in order for you to meet the necessary competencies.

- your supervisor and counsellor have responsibility with regard to confirming on your final assessment submission that your documentation is a true and accurate representation of your training and experience.

You must take a positive approach to the meetings during the training period to discuss progress. Make sure that you agree the times and dates for these meetings and are prepared to give your input. As explained previously, use the experience record as the focal point for these meetings. Remember that your final assessment will be based on your performance and competency statements and levels, and it is therefore important that your training and experience are geared towards this. The regular meetings with your supervisor and counsellor will be the ideal opportunity to review progress and to forward plan how you will fill any gaps.

Templates are available from www.rics.org/apc for progress reports to be prepared by your supervisor and your counsellor. These are not submitted to RICS but are a useful tool for recording the discussions at your assessments and your supervisor's and counsellor's views of your progress.

Summary

- The information and evidence contained in your diary, candidate achievement record, professional development record and experience record are very important. They will be used both by your supervisor and counsellor in their assessments and in the final assessment to satisfy the panel that you meet the training and experience requirements of the APC.

- Your diary must be available for inspection if requested by the RTA or the assessment panel.

- Get into the habit of completing your diary weekly, your log book monthly and your experience record and log book summary at least quarterly.

- The candidate achievement record comprises the log book and the log book summary. The log book provides details of the numbers of days experience you have had in each competency each month and the log book summary provides the number of days each year for each competency and the competency levels that have been achieved as assessed by your supervisor and your counsellor.

- Be proactive in all meetings with your supervisor and counsellor. Plan and prepare for them.

Preparation for the final assessment

This chapter covers the months in the run-up to the final assessment interview. It considers the paperwork that needs to be completed for the final assessment. In order to assist your preparation, it provides detailed guidance on the methodology that will be adopted by the panel during the interview. Finally, advice on preparing the final assessment record and the critical analysis is given.

The paperwork

You will have decided your target final assessment date with your supervisor and your counsellor at the beginning of your APC journey. The earliest date you can apply for final assessment is after you have recorded at least 22 months of experience for graduate route 1 or 11 months of experience for graduate route 2, satisfied the minimum competency levels for your pathway and undertaken the required number of hours of professional development and days of recorded experience.

To apply for final assessment: send your final assessment application form to RICS during the dates shown on www.rics.org. You will then have one month to complete and send to RICS your final assessment submissions. These submissions must be complete or you will not be eligible to take the final assessment. Once these submissions are received by RICS, you will be sent confirmation of the date, time and venue of your final assessment. You will be sent these details around one month prior to your assessment. There are two important points to note with regard to this:

1   if you do not wish to sit your final assessment on the proposed date, the onus is on you to notify RICS that you are deferring and this must be done before the start of the submission period for your pathway; and

2   if you have any special needs or disabilities, RICS will, subject to notification and medical evidence, take appropriate measures to assist you at the assessment centre. There is a box on the application form to be completed if this is the case.

RICS will match panels and candidates in terms of background, training and experience, so that the detail of the interview may be correctly targeted by assessors with experience in similar areas to your own. If you need any help or advice regarding applying for final assessment, you can contact the RICS Contact Centre (see page 121).

Alternatively you can contact an APC doctor for advice on the final assessment requirements.

Final assessment interview

This book has been written in a logical order, that is to say, following the actual course of your APC. At first sight, therefore, it may appear that consideration of the final assessment interview at this juncture is a little premature. However, this is to give you an understanding of competency-based interviewing, so that you can start the mental preparation for the interview at an early stage. In particular, it is important that you are focused on this concept in the two to three month run-up period in which you will prepare your critical analysis and presentation.

Structured and planned revision and preparation for the final assessment will be critical. In many ways the final assessment can be compared to training for a major sporting event. To be successful, an athlete needs to approach the run-up to the big event in a planned and structured way, looking to peak, in performance terms, on the day. You will need to take the same approach to the run-up to your final assessment. Put the time and effort in, and you will be more likely to succeed.

In the lead-up to the big event, you need to have a clear understanding of competency-based interviewing, so that you can take an informed approach to the revision and preparation needed for the final assessment interview.

All good interviews essentially have eight important aspects:

1   they are objective;

2   they have set criteria;

3   the role of the chairman is clearly set out;

4   they have a defined structure identical for all interviewees;

5   they adopt a robust questioning technique;

6   note-taking is undertaken;

7   they provide equal opportunities; and

8   they are undertaken using professional conduct, best practice and with excellent customer care.

This chapter will look at the objectives and criteria in terms of how they link to competency-based interviewing; the remaining aspects of the interview will be discussed in chapter 5.

The objective

The objective of any interview must be clearly defined at the outset. Interviews are conducted for a variety of reasons – for employment, promotion, appraisal or dismissal.

The objective of the APC is to ensure that only those candidates who have an acceptable level of competence in carrying out the work of a professionally qualified surveyor on behalf of a client or an employer are admitted to professional membership of RICS – simply put, to test whether you are 'competent to practise' as a chartered surveyor.

Your competence will mainly be judged by the assessment panel asking questions, many of which will test your ability to put theory into practice. Throughout the interview, the assessors will set questions based on everyday problems faced by practising surveyors. This is an important concept. The APC is a *practical* test and assessment panels are made up of practising surveyors who are best placed to test your competence – based on their own up to date knowledge and current experience of the problems, issues and difficulties faced by the profession.

The criteria

In any interview situation, it is important that criteria are set. The criteria are the standards or benchmarks against which all candidates will be judged. They provide the consistency and uniformity required to create fairness, and equality of opportunity, for all candidates.

For the APC, the criteria or benchmarks are in essence the competency definitions of your selected pathway. During the training period you will focus on gaining experience which aligns with the levels in the various competencies and these will also be tested in the final assessment. It is this approach that will provide the fairness and level playing field for all candidates.

However there are also some developmental criteria, which have a longer-term connotation. Management is a good example, as management skills and abilities, if nurtured and developed, evolve over a period of time, whereas certain aspects of technical development can occur more immediately.

With regard to the developmental criteria, you will be expected to demonstrate that you have developed so that you:

- are a good ambassador for your profession, RICS and your employer;

- are aware of the professional and commercial implications of your work;

- understand your clients' and employer's thinking and objectives; and

- have an up to date and developing knowledge of legal and technical matters relevant to the work that you do and the law of the region or country in which you practise.

These criteria overarch the whole assessment process. If you think of the objective – becoming competent to practise – as a mission statement, the competency definitions and developmental criteria can be seen as the detail that underpin that statement.

Additional criteria have been set for the critical analysis and the presentation, which will be discussed both in this chapter (the critical analysis on page 69) and chapter 5 (the presentation on page 85).

A competency-based interview

The interview for the final assessment is largely competency-based. The objective of this is to allow you to demonstrate your skills and abilities against the various competencies and levels you have achieved during your training period. Whereas in a criterion-based interview the interviewer would mainly focus on knowledge and skills, in a competency-based interview, he or she will also consider attitude and behaviours. The philosophy behind the competency-based interview is that past behaviour is the best predictor of future behaviour.

Bearing in mind that the objective of the APC is to consider whether you are competent to practise as a chartered surveyor in the widest sense, the assessors will test knowledge of a range of issues of general relevance to your competencies and your pathway, as well as seeking to ascertain your awareness of your limitations and your knowledge of matters of wider concern to the profession. On occasions, therefore, you may be asked questions outside of your actual training and experience. A good example of this relates to the Rules of Conduct – the senior partner or managing director of your firm will usually deal with many aspects of the Rules of Conduct, such as the client account regulations, and in normal circumstances you will not gain hands-on experience of such matters, but you will still be expected to have some knowledge of the basic issues.

The assessors may also wish to test your ability to take learning and experience in one area within a competency or a number of competencies and apply it elsewhere. In other words, they may test skills transfer – stepping outside of your actual training and experience to ask you to apply what you have learnt to a hypothetical situation.

The objective, competencies and developmental criteria will be drawn together by the assessment panel during the course of the interview. The panel will take a competency and start by testing against the levels shown in the definition and include some of the developmental criteria, with a view to addressing the objective of the interview: Are you competent to practise as a Chartered Surveyor? For an example see figure 6 opposite.

Figure 6 Questioning for competence in the quantity surveying and construction pathway

The aim of the assessment will be to test that you have attained the full range of competence required by your pathway. You will not necessarily be questioned in the interview against every competency. The evidence provided in your final assessment submissions will be used by the assessment panel in addition to the testing that takes place during the final assessment. Testing in one area may also draw upon evidence to support other competencies and criteria.

In the example of figure 6, the test of your ability to put theory into practice will also serve to demonstrate your knowledge of legal and technical matters, your awareness of the professional and commercial implications of your work and so on. Generally, you will find that in the course of testing your ability to apply your knowledge

65

and understanding, an experienced assessor will draw out details of your knowledge, skills and abilities in relation to a large number of other competencies and criteria.

At the end of the interview the assessment panel will make a judgment as to whether you have demonstrated the required level of competence. As shown in the example above, the panel will do this by taking any of the appropriate competencies and asking questions to ensure that you meet the levels and criteria that have been set. On this basis you will then be considered for professional membership of RICS, as the overall objective of the APC will have been met.

It is also important to note that in a 60-minute interview the panel will not be able to test a full two years of training and experience. They will need to be selective – so don't worry if there are gaps and omissions. The panel may have been satisfied by some other piece of evidence, in the written submissions, concerning your competence – it is not all down to questions and answers in the interview.

Having explained the basic concepts of the interview, you will realise that you will need to revise a range of issues that are of general relevance to your competencies, your pathway and to the profession. Below are some examples of when the panel interviewer may step outside of your actual training and experience in their questioning:

- Rules of Conduct – although you may not have hands on experience in all elements of the Rules of Conduct (perhaps particularly those for firms) the panel will expect you to have knowledge of the Rules of Conduct and of their implications on the practice of surveyors and their firms.

- Politics and economics – you should be aware of the general economy and the affect this has on property and construction.

- Taxation – although you may not have taken a specific competency in taxation you should be aware of general taxes and their impact on property and construction.

Other areas will depend upon your pathway and chosen competencies. You should discuss this with your supervisor and counsellor as they will be able to guide you in terms of issues that are of relevance to your pathway. APC doctors can also provide guidance in this area.

These examples should provide some guidance in terms of the background reading you will need to do in preparation for the interview. You should put together a timetabled action plan for your revision that sets out the background reading and research you will need to do and identifies the sources of information you will use for this.

Final assessment submissions

The remainder of this chapter will consider your final assessment submissions, in particular the experience record and the critical analysis. You should refer to the guide for submitting your final assessment submission, available at www.rics.org/apc, for further advice on the submissions. You will need to submit four copies of the entirety of the Excel workbook for your chosen pathway, which includes all the necessary templates, many of which you will have been using throughout your APC. The full set of templates to be submitted for final assessment are:

- Template 1 – candidate declaration – supervisors and counsellors will need to sign this template.

- Template 2 – candidate checklist.

- Template 3 – candidate achievement record – this must show compliance with the minimum number of recorded days needed and the achievement of the minimum competency requirements for the relevant pathway.

- Template 4 – professional development record – showing 48 hours of professional development for each year (see page 44).

- Template 5 – education record.

- Template 6 – experience record.

- Critical analysis.

You should also keep a copy of these templates for yourself. These same templates are submitted for all graduate routes (1, 2 and 3) and also for adaptation route candidates.

Experience record

The experience record was introduced on page 54 and will have been maintained throughout the course of your APC training. The objective of the experience record is to give the assessment panel details of the training and experience you have gained during the course of your APC. The information you provide should support the competencies and levels that you have achieved. Your record will give the panel practical examples of the work that you have been doing, to help them to properly target their questions to your training and experience. You should provide approximately 150–200 words for each level of competence you have achieved.

If you are a graduate route 3 or adaptation route candidate you will need to select your pathway and your optional competencies and prepare the experience record (or similar document) relating to your previous experience. You will also need to ask your sponsor to confirm that you have satisfied the competency requirements for your pathway, after which you must complete the candidate achievement record (log book summary element). You do not need to complete the log book or the number of days experience you have in the log book summary. Further guidance for graduate route 3 and adaptation route candidates can be obtained from www.rics.org/joinrics

Critical analysis

The critical analysis is a written report of a maximum 3,000 words. It is a detailed analysis of a project with which you have been extensively involved during your training period, with a conclusion giving a critical appraisal of the project, together with a reflective analysis of the experience gained.

The choice of project is very important as this forms a central component of the APC final assessment. Your role within an instruction or project that is considerable in size or importance could be an appropriate topic for the critical analysis (see the further guidance on page 71 concerning 'key issues') but equally a small, low value project in which you had a very hands on involvement may be a suitable topic. The project that you choose need not be particularly complicated, or of great financial value; it may simply be typical of the type of work with which you have been involved.

It must be emphasised that you are not expected to be running the project you choose. It is your involvement or role in the team that you are expected to outline, analyse and comment on. It is also not necessary that the project has a definite start and finish point – it may be that at the time of writing your critical analysis the project has not reached a conclusion, so your report will comprise the detail up to the date of writing, and perhaps a prognosis of the outcomes.

The report may be supported by appendices. However, it is quality not quantity that is important, so do not include too many, or too lengthy, appendices. Appendices may be included to support your report, not to add or expand upon it.

The format of the critical analysis is clearly set out in the APC guidance and it is important that this is followed.

One of the main reasons for referral is that the guidance has not been followed and that the format of the critical analysis is too similar to the type of report that you would write at work. The main headings of the report should be:

- key issues;

- options;

- your proposed solution; and

- conclusion and analysis of experience gained.

The assessors are also looking for good communication skills, so think about the layout of the report, the presentation and use of photographs and plans, the grammar, spelling, number of words, index, pagination, and so on. This is an excellent opportunity for the panel to assess your written presentation skills.

As the assessors are also looking for a high level of professional and technical skills, make sure that this aspect of your report is checked and double-checked.

Main report headings in detail

Key issues

The project that you have been involved in could be fairly extensive. If you select too many key issues, it is likely that you will merely skim the surface of them, rather than undertaking a detailed analysis. So be selective. You may wish to select just one key issue. Overall, to meet the requirement of a 'detailed analysis', think about the depth required as being about level 3 for the various competencies involved.

Options and reasons for rejecting solutions

It is uncertainty that creates the need for experts, and it is the diversity of solutions to any particular problem that leads clients to request professional advice. Therefore, before proposing a solution to a client, you will need to consider all of the options. Under this heading, you must demonstrate your ability to think laterally and must show that you have genuinely considered other options to your preferred solution. Give reasons as to why some solutions were not feasible.

Do not fall into the trap of going down one route only. The APC guidance clearly requests that you consider various options or possible courses of action and also that you give reasons for the rejection of those options not selected.

Your proposed solution

You must give a detailed account of the reasons
supporting your adopted course of action. Here again
it is important that your thoughts cover a broad
canvas. Too many critical analyses simply deal with
the technical aspects of a particular job. Think about
all the aspects that support your decision: financial,
technical and professional, and issues relating to
customer care, the Rules of Conduct, ethics and
conflicts of interest.

Conclusion and analysis of experience gained

The conclusion to your report must include a critical
appraisal of the outcomes, together with your own
views and feelings as to what you have learnt from the
experience. This part of your report may account for
around one-quarter to one-third of the total number
of words.

The critical appraisal is all about introspection. All good
professionals need to be able to look at a project,
consider what they have done well, identify what they
have not done so well, and plan how they might improve
upon their actions the next time they carry out a similar
task. Consideration of all of this will comprise your
critical appraisal of the project. It is very important that
your role within the project is absolutely clear to the
panel and you should, therefore, write the report in the
first person.

The next step is to stand back from the project and
reflect upon what you have learnt from the experience.

The assessors will take your critical appraisal as a
starting point to question you beyond what you actually
did and to probe your understanding of the wider issues

surrounding your project. It is therefore useful to start thinking about these aspects while you are writing your critical analysis, rather than waiting until you are in the interview.

You, your supervisor and your counsellor should provide a written declaration that the critical analysis is a true and accurate representation of your involvement in the project.

You must also ensure that you have your employer's and any client's consent to disclose any sensitive information in your critical analysis. If you are unable to obtain this then you should disguise any facts that might allow the panel to identify your project and you should advise that this has been done. All information in your critical analysis will be treated in the strictest confidence by the panel.

Report writing

This chapter will close with some practical guidance on report writing. With regard to the critical analysis, if you follow the ten-point plan set out below, together with the practical guidance covered, you should be well on the way to success:

1 *The objective of the report*: never lose sight of it! In the critical analysis, you are looking to write a detailed analysis of a project (or projects) with which you have been involved during your training period. The conclusion to this report involves a critical appraisal of the outcomes, together with a reflective analysis of the experience gained. Keep this in mind throughout;

2 *Brainstorm the subject*: brainstorming is a simple technique where you take a topic or subject and write notes, in no particular order, of all of the thoughts and considerations that come to mind;

3   *Prepare an outline and consider the appendices*: start to put your brainstorming into some order, using headings and important issues. Then consider the appendices that will be useful to support or shed light on the critical analysis. Do not fall into the trap of using the appendices to add to the volume of words; it is quality, not quantity, that the assessors will be looking for;

4   *Consider the use of visual aids, plans and photographs*: for simple reasons, photographs can speak a thousand words and you have been set a limit of 3,000 words for the text! But do think carefully about the need for and use of any visual aids;

5   *Stand back and review where you have got to*: are you still on course to meet your objective? Does everything look interesting and entertaining? How would you view the content if you were on the assessment panel?

6   *Write the report out in full*: start pulling the detail together, in terms of the text and appendices, plans, photographs, and so on;

7   *Once again review the report*: look at the number of words and be particularly careful with spelling and grammar;

8   *Polish the report*: think of an attractive cover page and give some thought to the index, and paragraph numbering;

9   *Test the report for potential areas of questioning*: don't forget, the panel will be extending their questioning beyond what you actually did, and will also probe your understanding of any wider issues surrounding the project. It might be useful to ask one or two of your colleagues in the office to read your

critical analysis, with a view to asking you some questions along these lines;

10 **Think about the objective once again**: has it been met? Go back to where you started and consider the following:

   (a)   have the key issues been made clear?

   (b)   have you considered the options and, in particular, the reasons for rejecting certain options/solutions?

   (c)   is the proposed solution supported by detailed reasoning?

   (d)   does the conclusion include a critical appraisal of the outcome and a reflective analysis of the experience gained?

The critical analysis is not an examination and you will have access to texts, references and a whole host of technical and professional references when writing it. It is therefore important to narrow the key issues down, so that you can write to the appropriate level of detail. In doing this, take care to ensure that the technical and professional references are to a high standard, as this will be an important issue in the eyes of the assessment panel.

In summary, the criteria the assessors will be looking to apply to the critical analysis section of your assessment are as follows:

● has a suitable project been chosen?

● have the key issues been identified?

● have all the options been considered?

● are the reasons for rejection of certain options clearly stated?

● is the preferred solution supported by sound judgment?

- does the conclusion contain a critical appraisal and reflective analysis of the experience?

- has the candidate demonstrated high standards of presentation including spelling and grammar?

- does the report indicate high standards of technical and professional skills and problem solving?

You will recall that earlier in this chapter the criteria that 'overarch' the final assessment process were considered. The above criteria clearly set out what the assessors will be additionally looking for in the critical analysis. Figure 7 below shows the mark sheet used by the assessors when assessing your critical analysis.

Critical Analysis Title	Notes
Suitable project(s)/process selected for the critical analysis.	☐ Met ☐ Not Met
Key issues identified.	☐ Met ☐ Not Met
All relevant options have been considered and reasons given for those options which have been rejected.	☐ Met ☐ Not Met
Clear explanation of and reasons given supporting proposed solution.	☐ Met ☐ Not Met
Conclusion and critical appraisal of the proposed solution and outcomes.	☐ Met ☐ Not Met

Analysis of experience gained, demonstrating the candidate's learning and development.	☐ Met ☐ Not Met
A good display of professional and technical knowledge and problem solving abilities.	☐ Met ☐ Not Met
Overall standard of: • written presentation • layout • spelling • grammar • graphics	☐ Met ☐ Not Met

Figure 7 APC assessor mark sheet – critical analysis

Summary

- You will have decided your target final assessment date with your supervisor and counsellor at the beginning of your APC.

- To apply for final assessment: send your application to RICS during the dates shown on www.rics.org/apc. You will then have one month to complete and send to RICS your final assessment submissions

- Make sure that you follow the guidance on applying available on www.rics.org

- You must advise RICS of any special needs or requirements for the final assessment interview.

- The final assessment interview is mainly competency-based, but do not lose sight of wider issues that impact on the work of surveyors within your professional group.

- Always stay clearly focused on the objective of the interview and on how the competencies and criteria fit together.

- The experience record is an important document, as it will help the assessors to target questions and lines of inquiry. Give plenty of examples of your work and make sure they are a true and accurate reflection of what you have been doing during the training period.

- Ensure that the format of your critical analysis complies with the guidelines set by RICS.

- Ensure that the critical analysis addresses the key issues of the project you have selected and gives reasoned support for your chosen solution or proposal.

- Give proper consideration to the critical appraisal and reflective analysis that is required in the conclusion to the critical analysis.

- Spelling, grammar, presentation and a demonstration of a high standard of technical and professional skills are also very important aspects of the critical analysis.

- Most importantly, ensure that your critical analysis meets the criteria that the panel will apply when assessing you.

The interview and presentation

5

This chapter sets out the standard components of the final assessment interview. It seeks to expand and develop your knowledge and awareness of the role of the interviewer, and in so doing, to develop your technique as an interviewee. The presentation is also considered in detail.

Components of the interview

Your final assessment interview will contain a number of standard components. After the welcome by the chairman, your first task will be to give your presentation to the panel. The panel will then question you on the issues raised. Afterwards, they will question you on your wider training and experience, in relation to your chosen competencies.

Overview of the interview

The interview can be described as an information-gathering process in which the interviewer's most important skill is questioning technique. You will do the majority of the talking. At the end of the interview, the assessment panel will consider the information gathered and how well it meets the criteria set for the interview. This in turn will determine whether the objective has been met, which will then determine the outcome – have you been successful?

Chapter 4 detailed the various aspects of the interview, concentrating in particular on the objective and the criteria. This chapter will consider the other aspects in more detail:

- role of the chairman;

- structure of the interview (including the presentation);

- questioning technique;

- note-taking;

- equal opportunities; and

- conduct, best practice and customer care.

Under each section, an explanation of how the panel will operate is provided, followed by guidance on how you can improve and enhance your technique, with a view to delivering an effective performance, i.e. a performance that persuades the panel that you are 'competent to practise'.

You should appreciate that every interview you face will be different. In the context of the APC, no two assessment panels will operate in exactly the same manner. Therefore, the information that follows is provided in the context of guidance only, but hopefully it will be helpful for you.

Role of the chairman

The chairman of the assessment panel has a very important role to play during the interview – particularly with regard to the various aspects of the chairman's performance that are aimed at assisting you. The chairman will have made contact with the other panel members shortly after receiving your detailed information and final submissions from RICS. He or she will have held a brief discussion with the panel members concerning various aspects of the interview and will usually have arranged to meet them before the first interview.

A critical part of the interview is the opening three to four minutes. During this period the chairman's conduct will be geared towards settling your nerves. The final assessment interview can be considered as an 'advanced role play situation'. Consequently, you will probably be more nervous than you would be in a job interview. You could argue that there is much more resting on the outcome of this interview, with many more years of effort having gone into the preparation and this being the only 'job' in town! Therefore, the importance of settling your nerves and 'breaking the ice' is vital.

Figure 8 is a simple stress management graph that explains this concept in more detail.

Figure 8 Stress levels during the final assessment interview

At the outset of the interview your nerves will be high. The chairman and panel members will aim to help you settle these nerves. Just before the end of the interview, when the chairman signals the close, your nerves will rise again for one last time. Your nerves may also increase somewhat as the interview progresses and you move from one panel member to another.

So how will the panel try to help you settle your nerves? There are a number of things they can do, such as:

- *introductions*: as soon as you enter the room, the panel will follow an agreed format in terms of handshakes and the provision of names and any relevant background information;

- *structure*: the chairman will generally give a brief outline of the structure of the interview. This will give you an idea of how the panel intends to organise the time and will help you know what will happen next;

- *comfort*: the panel will make you feel comfortable by offering you a seat, water, the opportunity to take your jacket off, and so on.

- *notes*: the chairman will explain that the panel may be keeping notes. Do not be put off, therefore, if you see the panel scribbling away furiously. This is done to assist with your assessment at the end of the interview;

- *health check*: after you have settled in, and before you move on to the presentation, the chairman may check to ensure that you are 'fit and well and ready to proceed' – or similar words to that effect. This check is to ensure that all candidates are given equality of opportunity. If you feel unwell before the interview, it is important that you do not proceed. You should tell the chairman, who will advise you what to do;

- *the ice-breaker*: the opening question asked by the chairman will be designed to 'break the ice'. The only way that you can get rid of nerves in an interview is by talking them out! The chairman will ensure that your first question is easy to answer and may be phrased something along the lines of, 'Tell us what sort of work you have been involved in over the last three months [or other period]'. Make sure that you are prepared for this question. Practise your response in advance, as this will help you at the beginning of the interview, when your nerves will be at a peak;

- *last word*: the panel will always let you have the last word. The chairman will say something like, 'At the end of the interview I will give you the opportunity to come back on, add to or clarify anything that we have discussed'.

The chairman may also provide the following additional support:

- keep you briefed at each stage of events, even though the structure has been outlined at the outset. This will help you with your nerves and will be designed to give the interview some sense of continuity. The chairman may use phrases such as, 'Thank you for your presentation, we are now going to discuss some aspects of it with you. My colleague ... will begin'.

Your role

There are a number of ways that you can help yourself prior to the interview:

- make sure that you know where the assessment centre is. Time your journey to give yourself plenty of time. Try not to put pressure on yourself by worrying about these things on the day – sort them out beforehand;

- if you have had any problems with the journey, or are unwell on the day, let the RICS staff know. This can be taken into account during the interview;

- look the part. There is no doubt that a good first impression will give you a mental boost and will help with your nerves and confidence; and

- rehearse your opening lines and prepare for the ice-breaker.

First impressions

Figure 9 shows how we let first impressions, which are often made in the first few seconds of meeting someone, form our views and opinions.

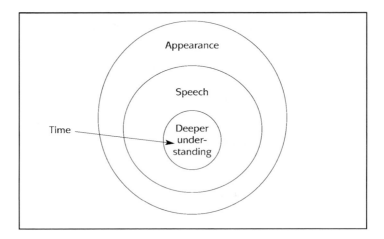

Figure 9 First impressions

When we meet someone for the first time, our initial impressions will be based on such things as stature, dress, deportment, etc. When the person speaks, they add to the mental picture we are building. We may immediately relate to the person's dress sense or accent, or may find that these do not conform with our 'norms'. We may therefore create a 'barrier', which can affect judgment and prejudice our views and opinions. It is only when we get beyond these first impressions that we really get to know someone and develop a deeper understanding of them.

The assessment panel will have been trained to deal with first impressions. To counterbalance the effect of such impressions, they will probably take notes during the interview, to ensure that you are judged on your overall performance, rather than initial impressions.

Structure of the interview

A well-structured interview has certain advantages. It will:

- provide order and discipline;

- help the panel cover the agenda – nothing will be missed;

- assist the panel with time-keeping; and

- provide a focus to proceedings.

You will probably find that the interview will start with a brief welcome and settling-in period. The chairman will then ask you to give your presentation. This will be followed by approximately ten minutes of questions on the issues raised. Following this, the panel will move on to consider your wider areas of training and experience in relation to your chosen competencies, with the chairman and assessors taking it in turn to question you. This part of the interview may last for up to 35 minutes. The chairman will then spend a few minutes closing the interview and will give you the opportunity to have the last word.

Presentation

Your presentation will be based on your critical analysis. The objective of the presentation is to give the panel an outline of the purpose, investigations and conclusions concerning the work detailed in this report. It should last for ten minutes.

You should not simply read from a prepared speech. The panel will judge you on your personal communication and presentation skills, as well as on the content of the presentation itself.

You will be allowed either to sit or stand for your presentation. The panel will not, in normal circumstances, interrupt you during the ten minutes, although the chairman may let you know that you are approaching the end of your allotted time – indicating that you should begin to draw your presentation to a close.

You should note that presentation aids, such as overhead projectors and screens will not be available at the assessment centre. Laptops are not generally appropriate for this type of presentation – consider the use of flipcharts that will fit on the table or perhaps just a short handout or simply some prompt cards for yourself. The presentation is more of a 'sit opposite and talk you through' than a 'stand and present to a large audience using IT' type of situation. And after all it is your personal presentation skills and the ability to communicate that is being assessed. After your presentation a ten-minute slot is allocated for questions relating to your critical analysis and to your presentation. The chairman may simply set the scene and then split the time 50:50 between the two panel members, or he or she may also wish to ask some questions, and will allocate time to do this.

Criteria applied by the panel

A further series of criteria have been set to assess this part of the interview. During your presentation, you will be expected to demonstrate:

- good oral communication;

- presentation skills, i.e. eye contact, the appropriate use of body language, and voice projection, visual aids (if you use any); and

- clarity of thought (that is, your presentation should have a good structure).

Figure 10 shows the APC assessment panel mark sheet for the presentation.

Oral communication skills	☐ Met ☐ Not Met
Clarity of thought and structure	☐ Met ☐ Not Met
Presentation skills: • eye contact • body language • voice projection • visual aids (if any)	☐ Met ☐ Not Met

Figure 10 APC assessment panel mark sheet – presentation

The above summarises how the panel will operate and what they are looking for. Consider the following when preparing for your presentation:

1 *preparation and rehearsal*: prepare, plan and rehearse. You might like to write your presentation out in full to learn from and then take prompts with you for use on the day. Rehearse in front of colleagues, family and friends. Ensure that the first time you give your presentation is not at your final assessment. You've got plenty of time to prepare, so make sure that you can deliver it backwards, standing on your head, in 9 minutes and 59 seconds!;

2 *structure*: think about the structure of your presentation and break it down into manageable chunks.

Consider the following five 'Ps':

- position: introduction – your name and outline of project, etc.;
- problem: key issues specific to the task;
- possibilities: lateral thought, options, why some options were rejected, etc.;
- proposal: option adopted, critical appraisal, lessons learnt and closing remarks; and
- preparation: forward plan before the day, and rehearse, rehearse, rehearse!

You will note that the above fits neatly in with the structure of the critical analysis. By following this structure you should achieve the 'clarity of thought' criterion that the panel is looking for;

3 *make the presentation interesting*: you only have ten minutes, so do not laboriously repeat the details of a property, its construction, and so on. Get down to the problems and your solutions, i.e. the things that will interest the panel;

4 *the audience*: it is important that you consider your audience. Think about how you will manage proceedings, the possible use of a short handout, and so on and also remember that your audience are 'informed' – they do not need to know detailed general background that a practising surveyor would know anyway;

5 *key sentences*: use sign-posting at the beginning and end of each section of the presentation. For example, 'I would like to start by giving the panel a brief overview of my presentation' and 'That concludes my opening remarks and I am now going to move on to the key issues and problems that I was faced with ...';

6 *pauses*: don't race through the presentation at high speed. Think about your pace and use pauses to

denote the natural breaks in the structure and to signify the next chunk or section of your text;

7 *visual aids*: have a series of bullet points to jog your memory on a single sheet of paper or, if you need a little more, write the main headings with a series of bullet points underneath on postcards, which you can flick through during the presentation. You might also find a desktop flipchart useful. Using ten prompt cards (one for each minute) can be a useful way to keep to time – just remember to fasten the cards together in case of trembling hands on the day!;

8 *body language, voice and eye contact*: whether you sit or stand is a very personal decision. When making your decision whether to sit or stand bear in mind that the rooms are generally quite small and the panel will sit behind a table. You should, however, make this decision before arriving for your interview in order to save any indecision on the day. You should practise your presentation in advance in a similar situation to see how you will feel standing or sitting. Think of how you use your voice in terms of volume, pace and tone to emphasise issues or changes in direction. Eye contact is also important. If you are working from notes, make sure that you keep looking up and making eye contact with the chairman. Every once in a while let your eye contact 'sweep' the other assessors;

9 *your appearance*: don't forget to dress for success. Make sure that you feel confident as you walk through the door into the interview.

10 *make it personal*: speak in the first person and be very clear what your involvement was throughout the project.

Questioning technique

Questioning technique is a key issue in any interview. It is through questioning that the interviewer will gather the information needed to make a decision, based on the criteria, as to whether to employ, promote, dismiss, or in this case, pass the APC. It is important that you understand how the interviewer will operate and what techniques will be employed. Therefore this section provides an insight into the various skills that will be exercised by an interviewer.

During the course of the interview the assessors will mainly use open questions. An open question is generally where a sentence starts with the words: what, why, when, how, where or who. This allows you to expand upon your answers and provide the information that is required to assess your competence.

There may be occasions when the interviewer will use closed questions. A closed question will elicit a yes/no or one-word type of answer and will be used to clarify facts or information.

Assessors will ensure that questions are well-phrased, unambiguous and concise. They will usually ask one question at a time and use short scenarios and narratives to help you understand the question. Supplementary questions will be used to probe and test your problem-solving ability and depth of knowledge. They may also be used to help and encourage you in moments of difficulty.

Think in terms of three progressive levels of questioning:

- *level 1*: tests your knowledge and understanding of the theory behind any of the competencies;

- *level 2*: tests your knowledge and understanding in the context of the application of this theory to normal practical situations. Assessors will do this by targeting your training and experience;

- *level 3*: concerns your experience and ability to provide reasoned advice and reports to clients. There may also be reference to more advanced technical issues. This will be done with regard to your experience, but there may be elements of questioning at this level that are outside your direct training and experience. This is covered in more detail below.

As an example, the following is a typical line of questioning from the rural pathway. It is based on the agriculture competency (T002):

- 'I notice from your experience that you have carried out a rental valuation of Quarry Hill Farm. How did you go about the inspection, particularly in relation to the farm buildings, land and crops?' (level 1);

- 'In preparing your valuation, and over and above these physical factors, what part did budgets and profitability play? How did these matters affect your thinking and approach to the valuation?' (level 2);

- 'I note that your client in the situation was trading at a loss. What factors did you consider or look at before advising on how to proceed with changing the business in terms of crops grown, overheads, marketing and general management?' (level 3).

An alternative approach to level 3 might test the provision of advice to the client:

- 'What issues and headings did you cover in your valuation report to the client?'

Be aware that if you have achieved a competency (as assessed by your supervisor and counsellor) to level 1 or 2, the assessors' questioning will not probe beyond that point. However, don't forget you may be tested outside of your main areas of training and experience within and beyond some of your competencies.

The phrasing and approach to questions that are purely targeting an area of competency may be as follows:

- 'Give me an example of...'

- 'I see from your experience record that you have...'

- 'What was your role/involvement in...?'

- 'Outline the process/procedures that you employed/adopted...'

- 'What problems did you encounter...and how did you solve them...?' 'What was the outcome...?'

- 'What did you learn...?'

Problem solving and learning is a key feature of competency-based interviewing, so be prepared for this line of questioning.

The questions relating to 'stepping outside' of your experience may be phrased as follows:

- 'What would you do differently next time...?'

- 'How would you apply this experience in tackling...?'

- 'What if a situation/problem arose...?'

- 'You have not had specific experience of...so in theory how would you...?'

- 'Where might you seek further advice and guidance...?'

This approach is very much geared to the 'big picture' so far as the objective of the APC is concerned – assessing that you are 'competent to practise'. It looks to test skills transfer and to assess your ability to take learning and experience in one area of practice and apply it to another. In addition, it seeks to establish that you are aware of your limitations – hence the line of questioning concerning seeking further advice and guidance.

The above outlines the approach to questions relating to the core and optional competencies. You should also be aware of the approach that will be adopted to test the mandatory competencies.

Ordinarily, when testing mandatory competencies, the assessors will refer to your past experience, rather than adopting a theoretical, textbook approach. Because of time constraints in the final assessment interview, assessors have been advised to keep the time spent on these competencies in proportion. A large part of the interview will be devoted to the technical aspects of the core and optional competencies. You will find that very often the demonstration of your ability in the mandatory competencies will be woven into the main fabric of the interview, and will be drawn out of your responses to the technical questioning in your core and optional competencies, as well as from your written reports and presentation.

However, there will be occasions when you will face some specific questioning. A typical approach is for the panel to target the professional development that you have carried out in order to develop knowledge and understanding at level 1 in any of the mandatory competencies.

Some examples of questioning approaches are as follows:

- What procedures does your firm have in place to ensure the delivery of high quality client care? (level 1);

- From your experience of ... can you provide an example of how you have applied one of these principles? (level 2);

- What do you consider to be the key components of a good presentation (or negotiation)? (level 1);

- Give the panel an example of a recent negotiation, how did you prepare, what was the outcome? And how did you judge success? (level 2);

- What do you understand to be the key principles involved in successful team working? (level 1).

Figure 11 is a representation of the APC assessment panel mark sheet for the interview.

	Notes
Attach the Achievement Record – Log Book Summary pages ONLY (Template 3). Relate your marking to the competencies noted in Template 3.	
Mandatory competencies	☐ Met ☐ Not Met
Technical Core competencies	☐ Met ☐ Not Met
Technical Optional competencies	☐ Met ☐ Not Met
Rules of Conduct/Ethics	☐ Met ☐ Not Met
Professional development	☐ Met ☐ Not Met

Figure 11 APC assessment panel mark sheet – interview

Interviewee technique

A useful ten-point guide for you as an interviewee is:

1 *ice-breaker*: make sure that you prepare for the ice-breaker in advance. Give it some thought and use it to provide the panel with some further insight into your training and experience;

2 *pause for thought*: before responding to questions, always pause for thought. The panel will not be expecting you to leap into answers. Always stand

back for a moment, consider the question, collect your thoughts and then deliver your response – look before you leap;

3   *active listening*: think of listening in an interview as an active, rather than a passive, skill, and make sure you concentrate on what is being said. In an examination, you would read a question and then read it again, to stimulate and recall information relevant to the subject. In an interview, you will usually have only one chance to hear the question, so practise repeating the words in your mind as it is being asked by the assessor. This will help you commit the question to memory and assist your powers of recall when answering it;

4   *repeat the question*: if you are not entirely sure what the question was, ask the assessor to repeat it. This is a useful technique to employ if you are asked a long-winded and complicated question – it will force the assessor to revisit the phrasing of the question and may help to focus your thoughts. However, you should do this only sparingly;

5   *chronological order*: think about chronology when giving your response. A lot of the questions you will be asked will command a response with a natural chronological order, for example, relating to techniques employed or the order of carrying out a particular task or function. This will help you collect your thoughts and ensure that you do not miss any important aspects of the response required;

6   *key issues*: if there is no chronological order inherent in your response, you may prefer to think of your answer in terms of key issues or bullet points. In this respect, you may find it helpful to use the various competency statements as a guide to your preparation for the interview. These statements will provide the trigger for the areas of questioning by the panel;

7   *unfamiliar areas of experience*: in the interview you will be asked questions outside of your main areas of experience. In these instances, do not be afraid to qualify your response. Don't forget, the assessor may have placed you outside of your main areas of experience in order to test how well you can draw from these areas and apply your learning and knowledge to an unfamiliar territory. Make sure you qualify your answers by indicating whether you have only limited or no experience in any particular subject area;

8   *mental blocks*: everyone suffers from nerves during an interview situation. There may be occasions when you have a complete mental block or stumble with the answer. Don't worry, the panel are trained to help you in these situations, for instance, by giving you more time, or approaching a question from a different angle. You will also be offered the opportunity to return to areas of questioning at the end of the interview;

9   *bluffing*: do not try to bluff or waffle your way through any of the answers. The assessors will all be experienced surveyors and will probably detect when you are unsure or are attempting to guess the answers. Often, when we are unsure in an interview, our body language or tone of voice can be a give-away. Bluffing will also give a bad impression in terms of duty of care and being aware of your limitations. If you are not sure of an issue, or really have no idea of the response required, simply tell the panel;

10 *final word*: you will be offered the last word by the chairman when the interview is drawing to a close. At this stage only re-open an area of questioning if it is absolutely vital. Close the interview by thanking the assessors for their time, smile and leave the room.

Note taking

The assessors may take brief notes during the interview, to ensure that they are being fair to candidates. Do not be unnerved by this. It is being done for your benefit, to ensure that the interview is a fair and impartial assessment of your performance.

The notes taken will, in the final analysis, assist assessors in considering whether to pass or refer you. In the event of a referral, the notes will be an invaluable source of information and guidance for you.

Equal opportunities

The need to be conscious of equal opportunities crops up in many aspects of the final assessment process. The following is a summary of the main points:

- the assessors will keep a record of the interview;

- the chairman will handle the opening five minutes with great care to help settle your nerves;

- the chairman will ensure that you are 'fit and well and ready to proceed'. He or she will check that you are not suffering from ill health;

- the chairman should control time across the interview as a whole and within the various components;

- the assessors will link questions to your training and experience in terms of the mandatory, core and optional competencies;

- questioning will mainly relate to the competencies and criteria set down for the APC; and

- the chairman will give you the last word before drawing the interview to a close.

Conduct, best practice and customer care

The panel will think of you as its 'customer' and consider 'best practice' to be about the delivery of excellent customer care. The preparation beforehand, the tone of voice used when asking questions and the way that the assessors look at you during the interview will all affect how you feel and therefore perform.

In an interview situation, these matters are important to both the interviewer and interviewee. Let us now consider some of these issues from both sides of the interview table:

- *room layout*: the chairman will ensure that the environment within which the interview takes place is prepared to your advantage. He or she will ensure, for example, that you will not be staring into the sun. The chairman will check that the panel have name cards in front of them so that you are not forced to try to remember names from the introductions. Before you enter the room, think about how you will greet the panel. As soon as you enter the room, decide where you will put your plans, papers, etc.;

- *eye contact*: you must always remain attentive and appear interested. However, do not spend the whole time 'eyeballing' the chairman or one of the assessors. Try to think about looking just over the interviewer's left shoulder, right shoulder or just below the chin. This will take the sting out of the eye contact, but will still signal to the panel that you are focused and attentive;

- *attentiveness*: sixty minutes is a long time to remain attentive. It is easy to gaze out of the window for a few minutes, read from some of the details in front of you, or fidget. Stay conscious of the impact that such actions may have on the panel;

- *body language*: you must be aware of the impact that body language can have on your performance. Be conscious of your facial expressions – a pained look may immediately convey the impression that you are finding an area of questioning difficult. Never underestimate the importance of a smile in terms of building a rapport with the panel. Also think about how you sit – avoid sitting with your arms folded, or leaning forward, eyeball to eyeball, and speaking in a harsh or agitated tone of voice. This will not give the panel a good opinion of you;

- *voice projection*: your tone needs to be warm and enthusing, the volume positive and confident and the pace such that the panel is able to follow and understand your answers;

- *listening skills*: your ability to listen and concentrate during the course of an interview is important for two reasons. First, to ensure that you interpret the interviewer's questions correctly; and second, to help you convey interest and attention through positive body language;

- *closing the interview*: before drawing the interview to a close, the chairman will ask if you have anything else to say. This opportunity will be kept within the parameters of the interview. The chairman might say, 'Is there anything we have discussed that you would like to add to or clarify?', thereby avoiding re-opening the interview on an entirely new topic. After this, the chairman will probably say, 'The interview is now finished. Thank you for attending'. He or she will stand, perhaps give a final shake of the hands, and gesture or lead you to the door. It is important that you leave on a positive note, so try to smile and don't forget to say thank you.

Summary

- An interview is an information-gathering process, with the aim being to provide the interviewer with the information that will satisfy the objective of the interview.

- Rehearse your opening lines so that you get off to a good start. This will help with your nerves.

- Dress for success. If you look good, you will also feel good.

- If you are unwell, advise the RICS staff at the assessment centre, who will provide you with any assistance required.

- Practise your presentation extensively before the day, so that you can deliver it with confidence.

- In discussion with your supervisor, counsellor or colleagues, try to anticipate the questions that may be asked on your presentation.

- Focus on the criteria that have been set for your presentation: good oral communication skills, presentation skills and clarity of thought.

- Understand the difference between open and closed questions and practise responses that make use of chronological order or summarise key points.

- Practise active listening.

- Use the competency statements and guidance on pathways while preparing and revising for the interview. These statements will act as the focal point for the questions from the panel.

- Do not be put off by the panel taking notes. This is for your benefit, to ensure that the final assessment is fair and is based upon the evidence presented by you.

- At the end of the interview always smile and thank the panel for their time.

Appraisal, referral and the appeal system

6

This chapter will consider what happens after the final assessment interview. It will look at how the assessment panel reaches their decision and will also consider referral reports and how you can make an appeal.

Candidate appraisal

After your interview the panel members will consider how the details of your training and experience have stood up to questioning during the interview.

As a starting point, they will consider your performance against the four broad headings that equate to the concept of being 'competent to practise' (see chapter 1):

1 core competencies;

2 optional competencies;

3 mandatory competencies; and

4 conduct rules, ethics and professional practice.

The assessors will link the mandatory, core and optional competencies to these four headings to arrive at their decision. There will of course be a great deal of overlap – for example, you will demonstrate your oral communication skills each time you answer a question. Figure 12 indicates the mental links the assessors will make between the competencies.

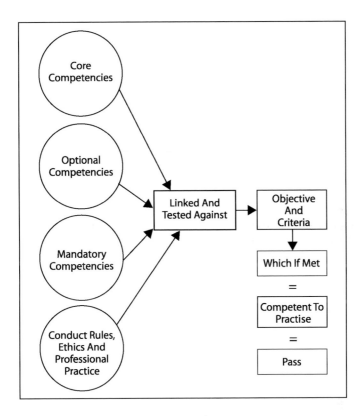

Figure 12 Candidate appraisal

It is therefore vital that you have a clear picture in your mind of what being 'competent to practise' looks like from the outset. Your goal should be to demonstrate these areas of skill and ability during your final assessment interview.

As well as questioning you on your training and experience, the panel will check to ensure that you meet the minimum training requirement of 400 days of experience gained within 23 calendar months (assuming you are a graduate route 1 candidate).

The panel will then move on and consider your critical analysis and presentation. These will be considered against the criteria set for these components of the final assessment (see chapters 4 and 5). Finally, they will consider your experience record. They will also check that your professional development meets with the minimum requirement of 48 hours per annum (taking account of any allowance for part-time or distance learning study – see page 44).

Drawing the components together – the holistic view

The panel will take a holistic view of your performance and then make a decision as to whether you are considered 'competent to practise'. All candidates are different and skills will vary. Some candidates will show strength in technical and professional matters and perhaps be a little weaker with interpersonal and communication skills. With other candidates, the opposite may apply.

Role of the chairman

During the decision-making period, the chairman will ensure that there is a consensus of opinion and will seek the panel's final view. He or she will listen to the panel members, particularly with regard to their areas of specialism, and will weigh and balance their views to ensure that the final decision is fair.

Final decision

Remember that you will not be expected to demonstrate a level of knowledge and experience equivalent to that of an experienced practitioner. The panel's decision will be based on you having demonstrated competence to the required level, tested against the various criteria that have been set. The panel will not be expecting a level of knowledge equal to that of their advanced years. The panel will wish to be confident that you are a 'safe pair of hands', that you are aware of and intend to act within the RICS code of conduct, that you know your limitations and have a good, rounded knowledge and that you possess the necessary skills within your competency areas and in general areas of relevance to your pathway.

It is also worth noting that there are no quotas or pass rates for the APC. The benchmarks that the assessment panel will work to are the levels of competence required, tested against the various criteria set out in the APC guidance. All candidates that meet these requirements will pass the final assessment.

Results will be sent to you by first-class post within 21 days from the date of your interview. Remember to let RICS know if your correspondence address changes. A pass list will also be published on the RICS website after each assessment period. For security reasons, no results will be given over the telephone, by fax, email or to a third party.

Referral reports

In the event of a referral, the chairman of your assessment panel will provide you with as much information as possible. The panel will have been asked to give reasons as to why you did not meet the required levels of competence. These will be given with reference to the specific competency (mandatory and technical) and with a clear explanation of how you have fallen short of the criteria. You may also receive advice on further training and development that has been identified as suitable by the panel. You will also receive feedback on your professional development and on your critical analysis, presentation and interview. Finally, you may receive feedback on aspects of your performance that were satisfactory. The objective of this is to enable you to address any weaknesses before the next assessment and to be successful when you re-sit.

The receipt of a referral report will be a miserable experience. However, you must remain positive and focused. Go back to some of the key concepts behind the critical analysis, be introspective, learn from your mistakes and improve areas of weakness. You have had the benefit of the experience, so learn from it and build upon your strengths, to enable you to be successful on the next occasion. Be philosophical. It may be that you were not quite ready for the final assessment.

If you are referred, there are some minimum requirements that you must satisfy before you re-sit the final assessment:

- record further professional experience. The assessors will probably give you guidance on this;

- the deficient competencies outlined in the referral report must be signed off again when your supervisor and counsellor consider that the deficiencies identified have been fully addressed.

- undertake a minimum of a further 24 hours of professional development;

- write a new critical analysis; or if recommended, resubmit the original, suitably amended and updated;

- submit a copy of your referral deficiency report and professional development deficiency record giving details of the further training and experience in relation to the competencies and professional development undertaken.

Appeals

If you are unsuccessful and are in any way aggrieved by any aspect of the final assessment, you can make an appeal. This must be received by RICS no later than ten days from the date on your results letter. The details of how and when to lodge an appeal will be sent with the referral report and application for reassessment. (These details can also be found on www.rics.org/apc)

If you do feel aggrieved, consider the following points:

- it is very difficult to get a feel for the outcome of an interview immediately afterwards. Your nerves and adrenaline level will still be high and you will find it difficult to be truly objective;

- if you are still feeling aggrieved when you get home, sit down and write a list of the aspects of the interview that went well, and then make a list of the aspects that did not go well, noting why you feel unhappy;

- after 24 hours, go back to your notes and consider whether there are any aspects you still consider to be unfair.

When you receive the result, you may well be pleasantly surprised. So do not over-react to one or two aspects of the assessment that did not go so well. The tendency in a highly charged interview situation is to remember only the downsides.

Two examples of why an appeal may be made are:

- administrative or procedural matters: the panel may not have been provided with the correct information and detail; or something may have gone wrong, for example, denying you the opportunity to make your presentation; or

- the questioning and testing of competence concentrated too heavily outside of your main areas of training and experience.

Hopefully, such problems will not arise. In case they do, however, RICS has an established appeal system.

Appeal system

If you do want to make an appeal, it is important that it is made by you, and not a third party. You must make the appeal in writing, accompanied by the appropriate fee; and you need to clearly state the grounds on which the appeal is being made, supported by appropriate evidence.

Your appeal will be considered by an appeal panel made up of senior experienced assessors.

If your appeal is successful, your fee will be returned and a reassessment, using all of the original paperwork, will be arranged as soon as possible. You will be reassessed by a different panel and the normal rules and procedures will apply. Conversely, if your appeal is rejected, you will be eligible for reassessment along the lines of the notification that was sent with your referral report.

Advice and further guidance

- Be introspective and do some soul-searching. Is there anything you can learn from a referral to make you successful on the next occasion?

- With your referral report at hand, talk to your employer, your supervisor and your counsellor.

- You should also consider asking your employer to approach your RICS training adviser (RTA).

- You should consider contacting your local APC doctor for advice and assistance on preparing for reassessment.

- With your supervisor and counsellor, consider how additional professional development could assist you in addressing any of the shortcomings noted in your referral report.

Summary

- Ensure that your paperwork and final submissions are in order. The panel will check to ensure that you meet the training and experience requirements (a minimum of 400 days within 23 calendar months for graduate route 1), as well as the final assessment record and professional development requirements.

- In drawing the components of the final assessment together the panel will take a holistic view of your performance.

- The decision will be arrived at by considering the views and opinions of all panel members. This is to ensure a fair and balanced outcome.

- The panel will not be working to quotas or pass rates.

- If you are unhappy with the interview and wish to make an appeal, try to be objective. Seek advice from your supervisor and counsellor.

- If you wish to make an appeal, you must do so no later than ten days from the date on your results letter.

Conclusion

As we have discussed throughout this book the APC is foremost a period of training and practical experience. If you follow the guidance and ensure that you are learning the skills and reaching the levels of attainment required in the various competencies, you will be well on your way to a successful final assessment interview. If the training and experience has been correctly put in place over the required period leading up to the final assessment, the outcome should be a formality.

It is when candidates have not followed the various guidance that is available, and have not remained focused on the competency requirements, that the final assessment results in an unsatisfactory outcome.

It is also essential that you focus on the various skills required for the final assessment: report writing, presentation and interview skills. The practical guidance set out in the previous chapters should provide you with some insight to the challenges that lie ahead, not just with the APC, but for the rest of your career.

Finally, the following is a list of vital points to be borne in mind as you progress through the APC:

- Once you're accepted as an APC candidate, RICS will confirm your registration and give you a start date for recording your experience (RICS will allow you to back date your experience for up to a month provided you have been employed by your current employer for that time – contact the Membership Operations department for more detail (see page 121));

- if you change employer during the training period, you must inform RICS;

- the training period is a minimum of 400 days within 23 calendar months for graduate route 1, or 200 days within 11 calendar months for graduate route 2;

- professional development must comprise a minimum of 48 hours per annum;

- you must have achieved the appropriate number of competencies, and to the levels required by your pathway, before you are eligible for the final assessment;

- the final assessment is mainly a competency-based interview, but be prepared for questions outside of your main areas of training and experience. Remember, you are being interviewed to test whether you are 'competent to practise' overall as a chartered surveyor;

- stay focused on the competency statements for your pathway, particularly the criteria that overarch the assessment, as well as those that apply specifically to the critical analysis and presentation; and

- throughout your APC remember that there is a wide range of help and support available for you and for your employer, including:
    - your supervisor and counsellor;
    - APC doctors;
    - RICS training advisers;
    - the APC team in the RICS Membership Operations department;

- the RICS website;
- RICS Books;
- RICS Matrics;
- the RICS library; and
- other APC candidates.

One final point is that your learning and development never ends. Your professional competence will continue to be assessed by employers, clients and peer groups throughout your career. As the world around you changes in terms of consumer demands, law and technology, the content and focus of your learning and development will also change.

Therefore, when you become chartered, think of your lifelong learning or CPD as a vehicle to assist you with your essential and ongoing training and development needs, in a rapidly changing environment.

Index

RICS contact details and further information

There are numerous ways of contacing RICS and a wealth of information sources online for APC candidates.

RICS Contact Centre

T: +44 (0)870 333 1600

F: +44 (0)20 7334 3811

E: contactrics@rics.org

RICS website

The RICS website provides details on the routes to membership, how to enrol and how to apply for the final assessment. You can also download the APC guidance, templates, Excel workbooks and pathway guidance and find your nearest regional training adviser and APC doctor. Visit www.rics.org

RICS Books

T: +44 (0)870 333 1600

F: +44 (0)20 7334 3851

E: mailorder@rics.org

www.ricsbooks.com

isurv

isurv is an online knowledge resource for property professionals, brought to you by RICS. The *isurv* 'channels' cover a huge range of surveying topics, mixing expert commentary with official RICS guidance. Visit www.isurv.com

The *isurv* APC channel also holds excellent support material and provides links to information relevant to achieving each competency. Visit www.isurv.com/apc